AMONG THE
FAITHFUL

AMONG THE FAITHFUL

Dahris Martin

SICKLE MOON BOOKS

First published by Michael Joseph in 1937
This edition published June 2001 by Sickle Moon Books, 3 Inglebert Street,Clerkenwell, London EC1R 1XR

ISBN 1-900209-04-7

Cover shows details from a photgraph of *A Mozabite Family* © CORBIS

Designed by bk design, typeset in Schneidler and printed by GraphyCems.

For Kalipha ben Kassem, called Courage

CONTENTS

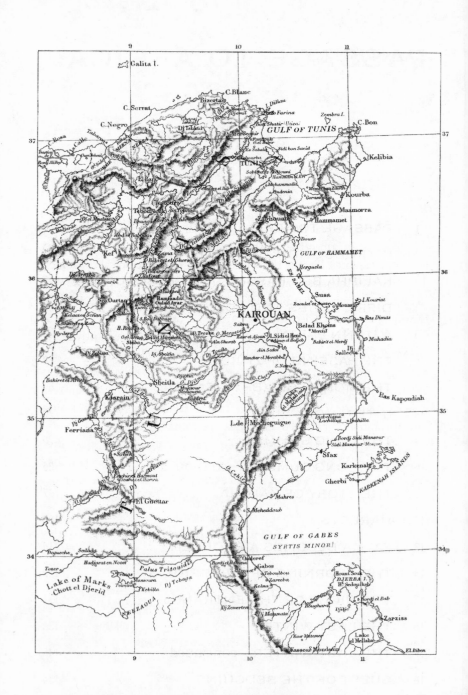

MAP OF CENTRAL TUNISIA

PASSAGE TO AFRICA

The perfect retreat from winter weather and worries! That is how the posters described the south of France. They mentioned hyacinths and pomegranates. 'Escape the winter!' 'Luxuriate in tropical sunshine!' The Riviera enthusiasts—almost everybody I met—spoke about the sun, the beach and winter bathing. The Côte d'Azur, they said, was just one continuous summer. I decided to try it.

October there fulfilled every promise. I knocked pleasantly along the Mediterranean and finally settled in Cavalaire, a village between Saint Raphael and Toulon. The Normandy *pension* was brand new; I was, in fact, the first to sign a name in the virgin ledger. Although the season was scarcely under way, Madame was getting a little anxious and made me a rate warranted to guarantee her at least one winter resident.

The trip south had diminished my funds alarmingly. I found, after paying a month's pension in advance, that I had almost nothing left. But, like Micawber, I persuaded myself that something was bound to turn up. There were royalties due me, the cheque would certainly come before the last of the month, and there was simply no end to two hundred dollars!

I was idiotically happy and as carefree as a dog. My letters of this period sound a little cracked. Sea, hill-towns, fishermen in striped sweaters and jaunty red pom-poms, ruined castles, *bouillabaise*—I doted on them all, and I simply couldn't say enough about the climate. 'This pension boasts of a central heating system,' I wrote 'I can't imagine why because this is "typical winter weather." Of course the evenings are a little cool.'

About the middle of November the *mistral* sprang upon this idyll. It came from the Alpine snow-fields—an Old Testament wind that called to mind Jeremiah's stern prophecy. For two weeks 'the voice of the Lord roared from on high,' the sea thundered, the sleet and the rain came down.

During the first few days I waited, from hour to hour, for the reassuring knock of the radiator. Gradually the realization was forced upon me that Madame had no intention of wasting her vaunted central heating on one unprofitable guest. Bereft of hope, I crawled into bed. I could not work, I could not read—I had purposely brought no books with me—so I crawled into bed with a French grammar, the most deluded wretch that had ever been decoyed to the sunny south of France.

I began to entertain serious doubts as to whether I had had any substantial reason for feeling so carefree. My purse contained something less than ten dollars (as a matter of fact I was afraid to count them), there was no certainty that the cheque was on its way and my month would soon be up. What then? I was trying to dismiss all this as a dark surmise to be dissipated by the first hot sun—when the letter arrived. There was no enclosure. The cheque was *not* on its way. Furthermore, I could not expect it until February! I lived through the rest of the *mistral* in a state of complete stupefaction.

The wind blew itself out at last; it remained cold, but the sky had cleared and a watery sun tried its best to shine. The incorrigible optimist in me was beginning to revive when I received word that an acquaintance, an American painter, whom I had met on the boat the year before, had likewise fallen victim to the Riviera myth and, in Saint Tropez a few miles away, was as miserable as I. Her blasphemous harangue against the weather—in letters two inches high—completely restored my soul. A crowded postscript proposed that I join her in a Thanksgiving feast 'Not that I have any sentimental regard for Thanksgiving,' she gave me to understand. 'The fact is, I have a primitive passion for savoury food which has been suppressed for a whole year, and mashed sweet potatoes, giblet gravy and turkey with sausage dressing are things I couldn't possibly forget. I can't cook anything, can you? To-night my meal was spaghetti and potatoes. I didn't know much about spaghetti so I cooked the whole pound. Well, I'll be eating it until you get here—and there may be some left for you. We might get a piece of ham—I don't think we can hurt that—and potatoes boil themselves. That will be about our limit on a two-burner oil-stove, and I know money means as much to you as it does to me.'

I decided that I wouldn't worry about money until after Thanksgiving. Madame agreed to roast a modest chicken as my contribution to the feast and, on Thursday, I set off for Saint Tropez. I found Beatrice at the top of an ancient building overlooking the harbour. Her studio was a dismal loft, as bleak and bare as a barn. There was a huge fireplace, but with wood at fifty centimes the stick, fires were not to be thought of, while the heat of the little oil-stove in a room of that size was negligible. The place was a tumultuous litter of shoes, palettes, books, canvases, clothes, paint-rags, luggage, fine prints, turpentine, food, brushes, and tubes of colour. An easel stood in the window, but I knew better than to ask about her work. It was said of Monet: 'He looks, he eats, he smokes, he walks, he drinks, and he listens—the rest of the time he works.' That was Beatrice. If she could not work she was sunk.

I located the cooking utensils (a misshapen saucepan, a frying-pan, one cup, two plates, a knife, three forks, and a spoon), and set to work on the dinner. It was, as I look back, a pathetic mockery of the traditional feast—canned peas, sweet potatoes, a little hard toward the centre, and a chicken that was indeed so 'modest' that Beatrice mistook it for a pigeon. Ravenous appetites plus a bottle of wine, however, redeemed all deficiencies. We lit our cigarettes, at last, more nearly warm than we had felt for weeks.

Presently Beatrice announced that we were going to have a fire. I cried out against such extravagance, but she had already bought the wood. 'Hell, this is an occasion!' she said, savagely dumping the wood on the hearth. Tonight, at least, we're going to be comfortable!

The fire was laid and lit, it seemed we could not get close enough to that first beneficent blaze. Then it started smoking. No matter what we did we couldn't stop it. We struggled until our eyes streamed and we could scarcely see across the room. At the sound of excited voices and running footsteps below we gave up. Beatrice flung open the window in bitter disgust and from the landing I shouted down reassurance.

'Damn it, I'm through!' cried Beatrice. Her fingers trembled as she lit a cigarette. 'I'm going *south*!'

I stared at her, bamboo huts and headhunters flashing through my mind. 'But that's *Africa*!'

'Well?' Her square jaw was resolute. 'Maybe you *enjoy* freezing. I'm going to take the next boat for Tunisia. And,' she eyed me belligerently, 'you'd better come along.'

'But I tell you I haven't any money!'

'Don't be an ass. I've enough to carry us both until you get your cheque. Living's cheap down there and we'll ship steerage. Kairouan should be marvellous!' Beatrice was pacing up and down, the collar of her cape turned up about her ears. 'A chaste white city—miles out upon the plain. Talk about your 'Mediterranean blue'—they say the sky is pure cobalt squeezed from the tube! And the sun! God, to be able to hold a brush again! To bake in *hot sunshine!*' That settled it.

On a sombre afternoon two days later we landed in Marseilles swamped with luggage, insufficiently clad against the raw wind that swept across the harbour. A bit uncertain about steerage 'accommodations' we bought a dozen sandwiches and some cheese. Beatrice added to this a bottle of Benedictine and I spent my last cent on a sack of ripe figs. Thus fortified, we followed our porters to a small deck at the very stern of the S.S.*Général Grévy*. They set our things down against the bulkhead. '*Voici une jolie petite place!*' said one, very heartily giving the other a wink. Fourth class, then, meant merely deck space, there was not even anything to sit on!

Sea and sky were grey; the wind cut at us like a scythe. It was only three o'clock and the boat did not leave until five. We were both panic-stricken. The harbour was crowded with boats: liners and merchant ships from Barcelona, Bombay, Istanbul, Alexandria, Singapore, and Melbourne. The vast thicket of rigging enmeshed us like flies in a web. Through the serried masts Marseilles was no vivid, impetuous, warm-hearted city; the gilded figure of Our Lady on the cathedral belfry was no gracious guardian of the ships at sea, but a destroying angel, swift and terrible. The air was a frenzy of flags and infernal noises; shrieks, groans, buzz, bang, clang, roar, and a raucous babble of unknown tongues: our desolation was complete.

We sat on the end of one of the suitcases and began eating figs and speculating as to whether a human being could survive such exposure for two whole nights and a day.

Our fellow-passengers (Colonial soldiers in khaki and red fezzes, several turbaned 'natives' presumably, in brown sack-like garments, and a solitary Chinaman) surveyed us with mild uncritical eyes, but we were objects of lively interest for the deckhands as they made the ship ready for sea. '*Vous êtes les Américaines?*' they asked. We admitted that we were. '*Évidemment!*' they told us smiling. Beatrice's paint-box, however, seemed to give us considerable prestige.

It occurred to us that it might be possible to rent a couple of deck-chairs, so the next time one of them passed I timidly broached the question. Pierre, we had heard him called, was a great, bearded, blue-eyed fellow, as supple as a cat. '*Mais oui!*' he shouted, nothing was simpler.

As soon as the boat left he would fix us up. '*Vous verrez!*' he promised, bounding away at a shout from the boatswain.

Above the mast-heads the riding-lights gleamed, the rigging had become a black impenetrable forest, the anchored ships had crowded closer. By the time the boat finally glided out of the harbour and the twinkling shore receded I was perfectly certain that we would perish. Even deckchairs wouldn't keep us from freezing. Then Pierre appeared like a genie out of the dark, smiling as if he had a secret. He took our luggage to a safe dry place in the stern. A few minutes later he returned, a chair under each arm. 'Follow me!' he said mysteriously and led us across the well deck to a sheltered dimly lit passage. Here he set up our chairs with a '*Voilà!*' No wind, no noise, perfect privacy, handy to the W.C.! If he had smuggled us into the glossiest stateroom aloft, Pierre couldn't have been more pleased with himself. 'What do you say, my little cat?' He chucked me under the chin.

There was simply no way to thank our benefactor. Beatrice undoubtedly saved me from embracing him by pressing upon him the Benedictine. He protested gallantly, but we insisted until 'to satisfy us' he tipped up the bottle and in a single draught half emptied it. To be out of the wind! There were no words for such relief. We spread out the sandwiches and took turns at the bottle. Decidedly, life was looking up!

We had curled up for the night—which threatened to be very rough—when Pierre popped in with a blanket. He refused to hear our protests, swearing with the chivalry of a *vicomte* that he had two, one for himself and one expressly 'for friends.' What with the plunging of the boat, the pounding of machinery in the room adjacent and too many figs we must have looked quite as ghastly as we felt, for when, some time later, I turned over, there, at my elbow, stood a huge, comforting wooden bucket! Such kindness—unsought and unexpected—was too much. I began to cry. As Beatrice was asleep, the hood of her cape pulled down over her face, I felt free to indulge my weakness. After a while I felt better and went to sleep.

I awoke next morning as someone planted a smacking kiss on my mouth! *'Bonjour, mon petit chou-chou!'* It was Pierre standing over me with a mug of steaming coffee. I suppose I should have been indignant. I should have upbraided him for his impudence, but somehow I could only thank him for that bucket. While I sipped my coffee he crouched on the foot of my chair talking in a low voice so as not to wake Beatrice of whom he seemed to stand a little in awe. He conceded the truth of the saying, a seaman has a girl in every port. But, he went on, it was not true of him, he was *pas le type.* Pierre—not that type. I managed to suppress a smile. He was looking for a wife, *une bonne petite femme,* someone who— At this point, much to my relief, Beatrice, blinking, looking a bit startled, pushed up the hood of her cape and Pierre sped away for another cup of coffee.

The sun was out, the wind was exhilarating, yet mild. Alongside of us, to the left, lay Sardinia, a reef of solid jade and rose-quartz, the sky, only a shade less blue than the sea, was filled with radiant cloud-galleons headed for France. We paced the deck, our chins up, rapturous with warmth. We felt we were aboard a boat for the first time in our lives, so close to the water we could feel the spray, in the very midst of the ship's work!

We were evidently the whole crew's concern, although it seemed to be generally understood that Pierre was our chief custodian. The boatswain put his wash-room at our service and furnished us with a towel and some soap, our chairs were dragged to the sunniest corner of the deck, and before the morning was over we knew all their names and most of their histories. Their French was almost as exiguous as our own for with the exception of Pierre, who was Marseillais, they were a heterogeneous lot including a Mexican, an Argentinian, several Italians, a Corsican, a Russian, a couple of Spaniards, and a Finn.

By noon we were so famished that we recklessly finished the sandwiches. It amused us that our rations should cause the men such solicitude. Nothing but sandwiches? No wine? No salad? They shook their heads. Very bad.

The cheese, which was to have been our last meal, was never eaten for when it came time for supper we were escorted down to the seamen's mess. The arc-shaped little room was lined with tiers of bunks and our friends were gathered around a deal table in a haze of tobacco smoke. They gave us a clamorous welcome, shoved over to make room for us on the bench and went right on with their conversation, all of them shouting at once, gesticulating and swearing—stunning expletives that meant nothing. Their arms were bare, their shirts open upon confounding specimens of the most complex tattooing. The soup arrived in great pails and we fell to. The floating cockroaches weren't discouraging Beatrice who kept pace, stroke for stroke, with the men; I determined to eat that soup if I died. I was the only one who was satisfied with one helping. There seemed no end to that soup! Long loaves of bread appeared only to vanish, fresh bottles replaced empties as if *vin ordinaire* could be hauled up from the sea. Tubs of French fried potatoes came next and buckets of salad with enough garlic to sink the ship.

Before we had finished eating, a mild argument between the Mexican and the Finn turned into a free-for-all shouting contest. On the assumption, perhaps, that we could not understand, they were oblivious of our existence. Each sought to yell down the others. For quite a while we could make nothing of the uproar, then, just as light was beginning to dawn, a strapping youth down the line floored the company by the announcement that he had lain with fourteen women in one afternoon and *'pas un gosse!'* (not a single child!). That was the climax. Nobody could match that feat. Things quieted down somewhat and they turned their attention to us. Where were we going to stay in Tunis? We hadn't an idea, did they know of a cheap hotel? Everybody knew of one and it looked as if there was really going to be a fight. It was Pierre who settled the problem. It was decided that we would stay at the Hôtel de la Gare. He proposed to write a letter to the patronne, with whom he was on very good terms, so paper and pencil were produced and Pierre, in the midst of an impressive silence, was permitted to compose his letter. We had been doubtful as to whether we could afford to stop in Tunis. However, if we could get a room at this hotel for six francs a night. Pierre's performance was acclaimed as a masterpiece. Introduced by such a letter Madame the patronne was not apt to overcharge us. We had definitely made up our minds to stay awhile in Tunis when Pierre put his mouth to my ear and whispered 'You will leave your door open a little crack?' My heart sank. 'Don't you think,' I said to Beatrice as casually as I could, 'that we'd better go right down to Kairouan?'

She looked at me. 'We'll try to make the boat-train.'

Late that night as we stood near the bulwark we were both conscious of a new quality in the air—a marvellous softness and—or did we only imagine it—a perfume, 'a soul-dissolving odour, to invite to some more lovely mystery?' The sky was peopled with multitudes of stars, Sardinia had fallen behind us, across the calm black waters there was not the dimmest light to indicate how near we were to land. And yet, it was long after midnight, and at dawn we would be in Africa.

INTRODUCTION TO
KAIROUAN

I t was still quite dark when the *Général Grévy* entered the Goletta Canal and the shore lights far ahead were indistinguishable from the stars. The quiet deck had been plunged into feverish activity, we had ceased to exist for the seamen scuttling to and fro, and I felt a vague regret that our passage was over.

The stars went out, the sky paled perceptibly, from the dark pile beyond the twinkling harbour definite forms began to emerge—ample domes, turrets, and the tall fronds of palm trees. Colour suffused the east, twilight shimmered upon the water, presently the sun came up from the sea and we drifted into the dissonant roar of the harbour. It seemed wonderfully fitting to me that we should land at daybreak. I was terribly conscious, as we waited among our luggage, that a period had been affixed to the life that I had known. A line from Wordsworth kept chasing through my thoughts, 'I made no vows, but vows were then made for me.' That gang-plank, down which the first-class passengers were already filing, was all that bridged the past. It looked so easy—ten short steps to a new world, a new epoch. I marvelled the thing could be done so casually. A poke in the ribs put an end to dramatization. 'Hey, wake up!' said Beatrice. 'Where's your passport?'

'*Américaines?*' The immigration official barely glanced at our passports and waved us on. Fezzed porters were swarming the deck, a troop of them fell to haggling over our luggage, in the end each seized a part of our belongings and bumped us down the gang-plank. 'We've got exactly twenty-two minutes to pass the customs and make that train!' Beatrice warned over her shoulder.

We landed in such a raucous rabble of porters, hotel-scouts, guides, and beggars that we were obliged to fight our way into the

9

building. After rounding up our baggage we hung around in an agonized sweat while the officials made their leisurely examination. With nine minutes left us we tumbled into a lop-sided victoria and simply tore to the station, and as the train pulled out the last of our bags was thrown through the window.

Battered, exhausted, we sank back, too relieved to care much whether or not we had all our luggage. 'Was your virginity worth it?' grinned Beatrice, pulling off her beret to mop her brow.

There was plenty of room on the benches, but most of the passengers preferred the aisle. They sat in tight knots, smoking and conversing,—magnificent bronzed creatures swathed all in white; from the stench of oranges and tobacco they must have been there for hours. The occupants of the benches were, for the most part, types less distinctive and striking. Their brilliantly coloured robes opened upon embroidered vests, their headgear was the fez or the turban, and most of them affected Paris garters and Continental shoes. A time was to come when I would be able to tell by the tassel of a man's fez or the coils of his turban his city as well as his trade or profession; now, however, it was evident only that our bench companions were town Arabs, from which we concluded that the others must be bedouins.

For quite a while we followed the shore-line, making prodigious stops at villages constituted, so far as we could see, of names made up entirely of consonants and of white, block-like stations. Camels in caravan, camels yoked to ploughs, camels pasturing, or turning ancient waterwheels, cactus hedges, olive trees, vineyards, orange orchards, and almond groves. After we left the sea we journeyed for hours over a vast plateau featureless of any growth save cactus and stubble, and enlivened only occasionally by a flock of earth-coloured sheep or a cluster of black tents.

We fell to discussing what our procedure would be upon our arrival. First of all we must locate the cheapest hotel in town. 'Do you mind bed-bugs?' said Beatrice. I did, horribly, but I told her I guessed I could get used to them. She laughed and said I'd probably have to. Then we must avoid guides. They would besiege us upon our arrival, but we would have none of them. Guides were stupid and costly; we were not tourists, we were here to work, and we'd see what there was to see during the course of a whole winter.

Just before the train pulls into Kairouan you are given a flash of it, a momentary glimpse of a dead-white city within battlemented ramparts. My heart was pounding as we approached the station. True to her prediction, we hardly set foot off the train when the guides accosted and strove to attach themselves to us, but in the face of every grace and stratagem we stoutly maintained that we had no need of them. Scores of urchins clamoured to carry our luggage, for a few sous we engaged a couple of them, and with the heaviest bags on their heads, we set out to find an hotel.

There was not a wide range of choice. The Hôtel Splendide was naturally out, the small Hôtel de la Gare, which appeared to be a roistering hang-out for soldiers, was crowded, much to my relief; we had no alternative but to register at another hotel. Madame the patronne emerged from her cups to show us our rooms, which were light and spacious enough, if not over clean. Then Beatrice asked the price. Madame, not too drunk to have sized us up for Americans, named one that would have been exorbitant for a whole suite at the Splendide. We had prepared ourselves for the usual contest. This, however, lengthened to a siege. At last Madame, with a gesture of accepting defeat, came down five francs apiece, and left us faced with the appalling fact that our living would cost us each a dollar a day. But since, for the time being anyway, there was nothing to do about it, we started forth to see the town.

The French quarter was negligible—pseudo-Moorish buildings on broad streets lined with stuffy palms and eucalyptus trees. Beyond the crenellated walls was the real Kairouan. A gate like a massive key-hole admitted us to the main street. It was broad at first and shaded by pepper trees, the deep fringe of which hung so low that camels in passing bit off garlands to munch along the way. On either side the mysterious life of the shops and coffee-houses flowed on, as ignorant of us as if we had walked invisible. We mingled with the traffic and, like chips in a stream, were carried along we knew not where. Donkey drivers cleared their way with incessant 'Burra! Burra! Burra!' from around a curve, or suddenly from behind a camel loomed upon us, loping along with an inexorable tread that stepped aside for neither man nor beast, a pack of shaggy goats scampered, bleating and bolting in and out of doorways, to the frenzy of the goatherd. Majestic Arabs swept by conversing with ringing voices and wide gestures, uncouth bundles of black or white drapery—veiled women, as we lived—brushed us, their bright slippers clip-clapping on the cobbles, and I could have sworn that one of them nudged me. There were women without veils, bedouin women who might have been struck from copper. They moved through the crowd like goddesses, their loose blue robes revealing now and then a breast or a lean thigh. Small girls with large babies on their backs simply *flew* past, clutching their headshawls and boys with school-bags contrived to walk arms around. A sound from another world —an imperious honk-honk-honk—announced a relic of the goggles-and-duster era packed with hilarious youths who had the air of enjoying that mode of conveyance for the first time in their lives. We had no sooner taken to the road again when a two-wheeled cart, as fantastic as a Czechoslovakian toy, loaded with turnips and pulled by a perfect giant of a camel, drove us once more to the curb. The street swung through the town like an S—at times it was broad, the shops set well in from the street, then it narrowed to a lane, and the very curb served as doorsteps. A sudden turn brought us into the heart of the town. I couldn't rid myself of the impression that we had come upon it at a time of carnival. The din, the swarm, the shifting colours of robes and turbans made it hard to believe that this was an everyday street scene. Here the shop-fronts were crowded with booths, and on the high counters turbaned vendors sat cross-legged fanning the flies from their wares, their cries jangling with the shouts of pedlars who strode through the streets bearing upon their heads trays of glistening cakes or loaves of bread. The fruit and vegetable stands, too, suggested fair day; it was as if a prize was to be awarded the most conspicuous display, but I couldn't take my eyes from the hideous little meat-stalls. On hooks above each block hung a frieze of staring sheeps' skulls. Scraps of gold leaf adorned the meat, the very fat of which was carved in naïve arabesques, and the piles of cloven hoofs and entrails could hardly be seen for the flies. Cats, grown enormous on butchers' offal, lurked about or slept on the sagging roofs, and the sight of them, combined with the unholy stench and the sickening hum of the flies, made me feel a little faint. The sun beat down upon our bare heads. 'God, let's get out of this!' Beatrice exclaimed. Casting about for an escape we spied an arched portal through which people were passing in and out. We dived through the door into a cool, shadowy arcade. Light sifted through apertures in the beams overhead and open shops occupied niches in the walls. Each cubicle was exactly like the next in its display of saddles, reins, and other accoutrements fashioned of dyed leather heavily embroidered; the stone step, on a level with the floor, was the customer's seat. Within the dim recesses the shopkeepers lounged at ease over their coffees, or sat on pleated legs busily stitching, conversing the while with competitors across the aisle. The street ended at right-angles to a similar passage, the street of the slipper-makers. The walls of these shops were bright with slippers of cherry red and canary yellow. The workers sat on low stools, noses fastened to their work-blocks, industriously stitching, fitting, pounding, clippng, measuring, and cutting like a bevy of gnomes with hearts set on shoeing the entire populace before sundown. One passage merged with another, crossed by still others, and if the footing had been precarious on the highway it was doubly so in the bazaars, where the passage of a diminutive donkey was a tight squeeze for pedestrians. From the street of the slipper-makers we drifted into the dignified street of the drapers, on through the street of the tailors, the balmy street of the perfumers, the street of the weavers, the dingy street of the smiths, the street of the carpet merchants, where bedlam in the guise of an auction rushed furiously up and down. We were wandering around in a futile attempt to retrace our steps when we hit upon an arcade that ended in sunlight.

Series of houses with grilled windows and doorways of sculptured stone fronted the quiet road, in which a tangle of lanes converged. With an idea of getting back on the main street we threw in our luck with one of them until it ended abruptly against the ramparts. The December sun was lowering when we came out of the honeycomb at the far gate of the city. The throng, pouring through the great arch, had gathered density and noise until, in the market-place just beyond, commotion had its climax. The jutting ramparts formed an amphitheatre that was swarming and buzzing with multitudes of bedouins, through whose midst strode camels in stately procession; sheep and goats were homeward bound from pasture, and for at least every other man there was a donkey; while seated on the ground, in danger of sudden death from every direction, were sand-diviners, beggars, public letter-writers, vendors, as well as bedouins in spirited *tête-à-tête*. The city wall was faced with rows of miscellaneous shops, booths, and coffee-houses, and separate chains of shops extended the entire length of the common. On the north side, deep within the shade of pepper trees, were the fragrant huts of the basket-weavers. The doorways opposite were festooned with earthenware and green and yellow pottery. We found seats on a bench under the trees, and a grisled old man in a pink turban appeared with a bouquet of long-stemmed tin cups. 'Kaweh?' he smiled, making as if to drink out of his fist. We assented rapturously, dying for coffee, never dreaming it could be had so simply.

The trees were alive with birds, the vast place swam in golden light and the white city, its turrets and clustered domes washed in rose, seemed about as palpable as a vision of the celestial city. It was good to be apart like this, quietly drinking our coffees. I realized with some surprise that we had landed only that morning, the boat, the trip, even the hotel, seemed a little as if I had dreamed them. It occurred to me that I was tired,stuffed, surfeited with impressions; even as I sat there watching the movement I wasn't relaxed. My eyes weren't big enough, I hadn't enough ears to take it all in, the things I couldn't understand tormented me, and while I strained for more, more, I craved a respite from my excited senses. I was about to announce that I was going back to the hotel when the beat of a tom-tom pulled us into the very midst of the market-place, where a circle was rapidly forming. The attraction was apparently contained in a hide sack which the performer, a cross-eyed wight with a head like a snake's nest, was opening with a killing pretence of caution. As he danced, and he never stopped dancing, his whole body swayed as if it had been simply thrown together. Now and then he would glide over to the bag, give a pluck to the strings, whereupon the little boys in front squirmed closer together. The bag yawned as the string fell away; the audience started chanting. Now the clown redoubled his capers, thrusting out his skirts shrilling 'Aiyah! Aiyah!' The snake slithered out in his own good time, erected a yard or two of his neck and raised his hood. 'Wah! Wah! Wah!' screamed the charmer retreating, then advancing, diving to scratch the serpent's chin, always shooing his skirts. The snake, his tongue flicking, wavered like a branch, as fascinated as ourselves in the demented dance of the charmer who suddenly grabbed up a tambourine and gambolled right over to us, shaking it suggestively. We each dropped in a franc, in addition to which four or five sous were tossed into the drum and, the snake having sneaked back into his sack, some of the crowd moved off. We turned to go, but the performer was before us convulsively swaying, exhorting us with eyes and arms upraised. Everybody was grinning. 'He says,' the Arab next to us explained in French, 'that good luck will follow you if you double the amount.'

'We'll have to do with two francs' worth!' laughed Beatrice. The Arab obliged us by making a reply that caused the charmer to smile and pat his chest and say *'Merci!'* Our informant moved away with us. *'Il'y a quelques personnes,'* he pursued, *'qui disent que le serpent n'est pas dangereux,'* and, with that, he told us a little story. A tourist, an American he believed, who stood right here watching this same charmer, announced, through his guide, that it was all *la blague*. The charmer, taking his life in his hands, showed him the venom-tooth, but the tourist carried on so that someone went for a chicken. The performance began all over again and, just as the snake was nosing out of the sack, the chicken was thrown down. The serpent lunged, the chicken teetered, flapped his wings, started to walk away, and fell over, dead. *Monsieur le Tourist* picked up the fowl, parted the plumage, and when he saw that the skin was brown—like chocolate—he gave the charmer five francs.

The pith and the amusing pungency with which the little anecdote was told excited our interest in the teller, and we accepted his invitation to drink coffee. With a halting gait he escorted us to the bench under the pepper trees. He seemed very well known about town. *'Hie Baba Courage!'* several voices hailed him; the basket-weavers, as we passed, looked up from their work to salute him, and the old man in the pink turban laid his hand on his shoulder, addressing him as *'Boyh Courage.'*

The face of our companion inspired anything but confidence. The chances are, in fact, that no Barbary pirate ever looked more like one! The swarthy complexion, the glowering thatch of black brow over his little bear eyes, the pendulous lips, and the baleful black moustache waxed at the tips—without scimitar or ear-hoops he was complete! His hooded cloak, which he wore *à la toga*, was dark maroon, the robe beneath it of black and mustard stripes. When he smiled his whole face opened, and what teeth he had were broken black stubs.

We both put him down as a guide, for he spoke French exceedingly well—or so we thought—and the things he told us of *'la ville sainte'* seemed obviously calculated to induce us to engage him. I had an uneasy feeling that Beatrice already regretted that we had accepted his invitation to coffee. And yet it was impossible not to enjoy him. From time to time, as she listened, her eyes lit up at some piquant turn of expression, for his speech had a flavour—altogether racy and droll—that Beatrice, of all persons, could not fail to appreciate. He knew that we were American, he

15

said, the moment he saw us. He seemed to sense, too, that Beatrice was a painter, for he told her of the friends he had made among sojourning artists. He had found them suitable lodgings, had secured models for them, in their purchases had protected them from trickery, had been to them, by his own account, guide, guard, and valet—sometimes even their chef. Here at last was an avowal. But then he went on to say: 'Artists are not tourists. The painter comes to work. He has no money for guides—even if he needed them. All he asks is a place to work. A piece of bread, a cup of coffee, a cigarette, and so long as he can work, what need has he of more?' Beatrice's eyes had narrowed. 'Then you are not a—a guide?' I stammered.

'No,' he said with solemn emphasis. 'I am not a guide.' He clapped his hands for the *cafetier*, 'but formerly I was a guide, the best in Kairouan,' and, as if to prove it, he pulled out a handsome Swiss watch engraved with a testimony of appreciation and esteem. '"Kalipha ben Kassem"—that's me.' I was on the point of asking why it was that he was no longer a guide, but something prevented me.

The sun had long set. Voices that seemed to have come from the sky had called the city to prayer. The market-place was almost empty, shops were shut for the night, and only the doorway of an occasional coffee-house gleamed through the dark. The *cafetier* shuffled towards us. Beatrice was for paying the bill, but our companion would have none of it. 'You are both very tired,' he smiled. '*Tawah nimshoo fluti*, which is to say, now we will return to the hotel.' He made us repeat it after him, again and again, until, by the time he took leave of us on the steps of the hotel, we had mastered our first lesson in Arabic.

KALIPHA BEN KASSEM
CALLED 'COURAGE'

Dead set as we were against guides, we had no intention of cultivating the acquaintance of Kalipha ben Kassem. But we did not reckon upon his perseverance! We could not take a step without him. He seemed actually to lie in wait for us. Sometimes he 'happened' upon us just as were leaving the hotel, at other times he came hurrying toward us from the French café near the gate, occasionally we had gone some distance up the main street before '*Mademoiselles! Mademoiselles!*' he would come limping up on his club foot. Once or twice we pretended that we didn't hear him. It was of no use the entire populace were in league with him. 'Papa Courage is calling you,' a dozen informants impeded our escape.

After sundry inquiries about our health, our work, our pleasure in Kairouan, he invariably had ready some irresistible proposal for our entertainment. We were undeniably the richer for these encounters, for with the good guide's unerring instinct he knew exactly the things that would interest us most. He took us to inaccessible coffee-houses where professional story-tellers held men spell-bound for hours, or where sloe-eyed youths performed the ribald stomach-dance to the noisy enthusiasm of their audiences. We walked outside the ramparts—the Holy City glamorous in the moonlight, our low voices trumpeting across the vast stillness of the plain. We visited the Street of the Courtesans, along the whole length of which our friend seemed decidedly well known.

Although Kalipha had the most solemn respect for our working hours, his knack of appearing just when we needed him testified to a constant vigilance. If Beatrice set up her easel in town he would stroll up as the curious onlookers threatened to block her vision and, without offence to anyone, keep the crowd moving. If he caught her in search of a model he scoured the marketplace until he rounded up dozens of idle bedouins for her to choose from. He was the mediator in our altercations with Madame. For every perplexity and annoyance, in fact, Kalipha had the solution. Kind, courteous, intelligent, infinitely entertaining, the only fault we could possibly find with him was his over-anxiety to be useful. There seemed no way to prevent him from becoming indispensable.

It must be confessed that my friend's sense of honour was more acute than mine. It would never have occurred to me that in accepting Kalipha's hospitality I was incurring an obligation that I could not possibly pay. Her anxiety quickly communicated itself to me, and we strove to make our position quite clear to him, feeling sure he would lose interest when he realized at last that his pursuit was unprofitable. He accepted our hints, explanations, and apologies, however, with a gusty sigh: 'Ah, yes, my friends, I tell you, the beggar in the shadow of the Great Gate is often better off than the artist.'

Who in God's name was this villainous-looking Arab who had appointed himself our squire? If he *did* know our circumstances, what was his motive in befriending us? How did he earn his livelihood? Although he had no visible means of support, Beatrice had to get really angry in order to pay for the coffee; if we stopped to purchase something he always succeeded in beating a franc or two from the price. Why was it that he, a born guide, no longer followed his profession? For over thirty years he had conducted tourists through the ancient City, held sacred by Islam still as One of the Four Gates of Paradise. His work had been his life. 'In those days,' he would say, taking off his well-worn fez, 'I wore the head-coils— cloth of gold, such as is brought back by the pilgrims from Mecca. It is not the poor man, you know, who can wear such a turban. As to *gondorrah*,' he fingered his robe, 'it was of the pure silk, a different colour for every day in the week, but always white in summer. I had not one burnous, but four of them. Camel's hair, you understand, very rich with embroidery. Oh, I tell you, my friends, when I walked down the street with my gold-headed cane, one might have mistaken me for the vizir to the Bey!' What had put an end to such affluence?

We were helpless to solve the enigma. Of only one thing we felt sure—he had been deprived of his license, whether justly or unjustly, by the French authorities. It was painfully apparent that he had no friends among them. Within the ramparts, he was surrounded by good will and affection. Men of all walks and stations—expensively dressed merchants, white-turbaned scholars and religious dignitaries, tradesmen and *spahis*, the Arab police, paused for the exchange of florid greeting. Wherever we went he was welcome, and as his guests we were bewildered with kindness. 'You are the friends of my friend,' we were constantly being told, 'therefore, you are, also, *my* friends.' But outside the walls—what a difference! The general attitude of the Tunisian French toward the subject Arabs scarcely accounted for the lack of respect that he, particularly, was accorded. If he was saluted at all, it was with a kind of cold contempt that used to infuriate me. Not that Kalipha was humbled! He always carried his head high, but when he stumped through the French town it was with a dignity that was downright majestic.

It was a compatriot—the only resident American in Kairouan— who explained away some of the mystery surrounding Kalipha ben Kassem. The year before Beatrice had met Mr. Bemen in Brittany where he spent his summers in order to be among artists. Off and on for the last fifteen years he had lived in Kairouan, where he had invested in land, olive groves, sheep, and camels. He was reputed, among the Arabs at least, to be very wealthy.

We met him on the street one day and he invited us to his villa. It was on the plain just outside the ramparts, a pretty blue cottage fortified by a high barbed-wire fence and a notoriously vicious bedouin sheep-dog. It was apparent at a glance that Mr. Bemen's hobby was native beds. The house was smothered with great nuptial bedsteads glittering with gold leaf and embellished in bright paint with all the symbols of fecundity.

After showing us his portfolio of dancing girls, he made an opportunity to warn us against our native companion. This was the story he told us. Two years before the president of the bank had been murdered. Kalipha's brother, Mohammed, and his friend, both porters, were found guilty and condemned to the guillotine. At the last hour their sentence was commuted, and they were dispatched to Devil's Island.

The Arab population, to a man, believed the prisoners innocent. Great numbers of them testified to their presence at an all-night stag-party at the time the crime was committed. The feeling against the French had been very strong, not only because of the conviction, but because Kalipha had lost his guide's permit for having steadfastly refused to testify against his brother. Bemen, himself, lightly admitted the probability that the pair had been victimized as scapegoats. But what was done was done. Whether innocent or guilty, the wretches were as good as dead now, and a couple of Arabs more or less, didn't make a whole lot of difference, eh, what? The point was, that Beatrice and I could not expect to curry French favour by associating with Kalipha ben Kassem.

It took me nearly a week to realize that I simply couldn't work. I tried desperately to get back to the story I had started in Cavalaire, but Kairouan had come between us. What with the need to justify my move to Africa in production, and the unsuppressible impulse to abandon myself to the exotic city, the drone of whose voice reached me in my quiet room at the back of the hotel, I was paralyzed. When the folly of the struggle struck me, I bought myself several thick notebooks and made for the market-place like a gnat for the light.

I was in the ring around a fantastic old tumbler when Kalipha found me. 'But, my little one, why are you not at work!' he cried accusingly. I felt, unaccountably, as if I had put something over on him. While I was explaining, he guided me to our coffee-house alongside the basket-weavers. 'But you are right!' he exclaimed, applauding my decision until I was amazed at myself for having wasted a week. 'The things we will see! For it is not by drinking coffee in the market-place or the souks that one learns the City! First we will visit the homes of my relatives and friends. I assure you, since you are come, my nieces, Kadeja, Fafanie, Zinibe, and the rest, break my head with their reproaches. Only yesterday Eltifa, my sister, demanded, 'What is your fear, O my brother, that you hide your friends from me? Search the house. Have I a secret cage where I could fatten them for the fête 'Here, then, is what I propose. Each afternoon, between the calls to prayer, we will distribute visits among them. That there may be no jealousy, it will be necessary to make the *grande tour*. And when they see you coming into the court, by Allah, it will be like the ascent of the full moon!'

I gave way with such spontaneous delight that Kalipha was jubilant and expatiated at great length upon our programme. In the meanwhile, I drank my coffee thoughtfully. He paused, at last, to sip his own and I became conscious that he was studying me. After a time he drew a finger across his brow. 'What is the meaning of that seam upon your forehead? What is it that troubles you, *hein*?' Confused, I did not answer. He hunched forward, 'I will tell you. To you and Mlle Beatrice I am a riddle: not a guide, but still a guide. A thousand times you ask yourselves: "With what are we to pay him? With the gold from our teeth, perhaps?" Listen,' he went on earnestly, 'my head is not a dry gourd. I was at the station the day you arrived. I am able to tell you, my friend, that when one has been a guide for half one's life one recognizes people. I knew you at once. Every mendicant that cries *Ya krimtallah!* for his supper is not destitute, nor is every traveller a tourist. This,' he said, picking up my change purse, 'does not interest me. I swear,' he raised his hand with impressive solemnity, 'as Mohammed is the Prophet of Allah, I swear that I do not want your money!'

'But, like us, you are poor,' I protested, 'we must all live somehow.'

'It is nearly three years,' he continued bitterly, 'since they saw fit to deprive me of my livelihood. I was guilty of nothing. Their own records prove the truth of what I am telling you. By Allah, there exists no man in this world—or in the world beyond—that I cannot look in the eye. Yet they condemned me and my family to penury, and but for the grace of Allah, who has blessed me with loyal friends, we should have starved.' He went on to explain that the merchants continued to pay him a commission upon the purchases of tourists that he inveigled into their shops. It was a dangerous practice, he admitted, for the authorized guides, who had long resented his supremacy, were only too ready to report him to the French authorities. By deceit and stealth, therefore, he contrived to exist, but Allah, the judge of the French as well as the Arabs, does not condemn a man for the sins forced upon him. To the present day, He had extended His merciful protection over Kalipha that he might gain his daily bread.

'And you permit us to rob you of your time,' I remonstrated, at which he threw back his head with such a roar that I had to laugh with him, in spite of my earnestness. 'My pockets are full of it! The Basha, himself, I believe, is not so rich as I when it comes to that! Ah, no, *ma petite*, you must not trouble your head. If I show you the things you would not otherwise see, it is because I have a pleasure in the company of artists. While you remain among us you are *musàfir*, which is to say, our guests. He who honours you finds certain favour with Allah, the All-seeing, but Unseen. And the face of him that dishonours you is blackened in His sight. See here! This night you and Mlle Beatrice are to dine with me.' He raised a warning hand against objection. 'I require it of you. As I myself will prepare the dinner, my son Mohammed will be at the hotel at half-past six to escort you to the house. Once we have shared the same bowl, my friend, there can be no question of money between us.'

'We will be happy to come,' I assured him from a full heart. I tried to add that it needed no dinner to confirm the friendship I felt for him, but, my French failing me, I gave him my hand. 'In any case,' I said, 'from now on, we are friends!' I was never to regret that impulsive gesture.

We supposed that Kalipha's son would be a young man. Promptly at the appointed time we were told that he had come. To our surprise it was quite a small boy who waited upon us. 'I am Mohammed, the son of Kalipha,' he announced himself, his dark eyes dancing, his broad mouth widened into the most engaging smile. He couldn't have been more than ten, and his chubby face in the peaked white hood of his burnous reminded one of a Rackham elf. Of his age he was not at all sure. Some said he was nine, his father said ten, but maybe he was eleven, even twelve. No, he did not go to school. He was learning to be a basket-weaver from Sidi Hasseen in the market-place. Our efforts to converse further with him were not altogether successful for, although he understood French, his inability to speak much constrained him to smiling silence as he slapped along in slippers many sizes too big for him.

From the main thoroughfare we turned off into a dark lane. *'Rue des Chasseurs à pieds!'* Mohammed announced with quite an air. A short, steep flight of steps led abruptly from the road to a narrow landing. At the fall of the knocker, there was a clack-clack of clogs descending stone stairs and the door was opened a crack to admit us. A girl held a lamp above her head. *'Asslemma!'* she murmured, smiling and patting her chest. As Mohammed seemed disinclined to introduce us, we asked him if she was his sister. 'She is Fatma, the wife of my father,' he said, unceremoniously preceding us up the stairs.

It was the first time that we had seen beneath the veils. Fatma's curly black hair was bound in a violet kerchief, over a kind of long-sleeved jersey she wore a set of embroidered jackets and vests. Her legs were clothed in full white trousers, a wide strip of striped silk wrapped her hips, skirt-fashion, and her feet in the pattens were bare. She lit our way to the court that was dark save for patches of light from pairs of low windows on either side. Mohammed opened a door upon a snug little whitewashed room in the midst of which, on the floor, sat Kalipha, before a fire-pot, busy with the supper. We left our shoes outside and, stooping to enter, we seated ourselves on a wide mattress that filled the end of the room. The stone floor was laid with matting, a strip of matting covered the lower half of the wall around the bed; under the shuttered window that faced the street stood a garishly painted wooden chest, there was no other furniture. And yet, as we afterwards learned, this one small room was dining-room, kitchen, bedroom and *salon*—in short the entire *ménage*.

Fascinated, we watched Kalipha in the rôle of chef. He was no novice; the deftness and precision of his movements suggested experience and skill. His street-robe hung from a peg on the door, surrounded with smoking pots he sat in his shirt sleeves, his legs, in voluminous white bloomers, pleated under him. Haroon er Rashid in the council chamber was no more the potentate than Kalipha ben Kassem in his own household. Mohammed jumped to his bidding, and with a jar in each hand, flew to the public fountain. Fatma, in constant attendance upon his commands, glided barefoot to and from the court. She was a strange silent little thing. Under an exceedingly low brow her eyes were deep-set and narrow, her complexion was pale, rendered more so by the black of hair and brows. She kept her face averted from us. Once or twice she stole a glance our way, but when we smiled she flushed, dropped her eyes, and covered her face in confusion.

'*Ya Fatma!*' Kalipha shouted at her, calling her to answer for some misdemeanour. Her mild reply from the court twisted his face into a horrible leer. Laying down his spoon, he folded his arms, and wagging his head, he gave a hideous caricature of her words and the tone of her voice, then, hurling the spoon into the court, he denounced her until I was wretched for her humiliation before us. But Fatma seemed not in the least put out, she came and went, serving him with the utmost composure.

'Ah, women, women!' groaned Kalipha as his wrath subsided. 'Verily they are devils! The source of all misfortune!'

When Mohammed returned, Fatma placed before us a tray on low legs, father and son took places opposite us and *cous-cous* in a great wooden bowl was set in our midst. Lumps of lamb and boiled vegetables—pumpkin, turnip, and chick-peas—were arranged upon the top. Although we were provided with large spoons, obviously purchased for the occasion, they were not displeased when we chose to eat in the Arab manner and showed us how to scoup up the savoury cereal with the thumb and first two fingers of our right hands. Kalipha warned us that it would be very *'piquant'*; it was like eating fire. There was no restraining our coughs and tears, but the tantalizing flavour and the hot bite of the pepper excited our appetites, and we kept at it. Kalipha's swarthy face shone with perspiration and approval. Mohammed, delighted, exclaimed: 'But you are *true* Arabs!'

We had scarcely made a dent in the great mound of *cous-cous* when Kalipha took the grass covers from several dishes alongside him. In one there was an omelette decked with parsley, in another a little ragout, both of which he had prepared lest the spices should prove too much for our untutored palates. In still another dish was a roasted fowl stuffed with rice, almonds, and raisins, delicately perfumed with amber. There was a crisp salad besides, and the dessert was an Arab sherbet, a pale-green, translucent pudding, tart with lime and full of blanched almonds.

Fatma did not appear until we had finished eating when she replaced the table with another and set the fire-pot before her master. For the next few minutes he devoted himself to the making of the coffee, an exceedingly delicate performance. Through the shutters of the window that gave upon the court we could see into the chamber opposite where Kalipha's sister Eltifa and her husband had their household. A still form in white sat against the wall; the frame of the grilled window, together with the soft glow of lamplight, gave the illusion of a reliquary in which reposed a priceless figurine in amber. It was Abdallah, master tea-maker and devout student of the Koran. Several years before, we were told, he had made the pilgrimage to Kairouan on foot from Morocco. The dearest wish of his heart had been to end his days in the Holy City, and as a reward for his zeal, Allah had instilled in the populace a thirst for Abdallah's tea, thus enabling him to settle here where he eventually married the widowed Eltifa, and was become a venerated practitioner of all illnesses brought on by the djinns.

We lounged luxuriously, it seemed we had never dined so well. 'Is it always the men that make the meals?' I inquired.

'Never!' he said with scornful emphasis. While Arab men choose the bill of fare and invariably do the marketing, sometimes even superintending the preparation of a dish, they never, never demean themselves, as he did, with the cooking. But what could he do? When he divorced Hanoona, the mother of Mohammed, he had made an oath that he would never remarry. For three years he had managed with the help of his sister. It had been a foretaste of paradise, a halcyon period during which he had enjoyed all the delights of women without responsibility or bedevilment. But Eltifa, who was blind, found his celibacy more of a burden, and urged her brother to take another wife. At first he would not listen, but she kept at him, like a flea in his garments, until in desperation he charged her, 'Search the city, only carry cotton with you wherever you go. And when they tell you that the daughter of so-and-so is a virgin with the beauty and form of the *houris*, stop up your ears. If, on the other hand, they tell you that she is neat, thrifty, and sober, that she can cook, clean, and weave, let her parents name their price, for though she be a *divorcée* and as ugly as a toad, this woman is my choice.'

Unlike the average Arab wife that seldom sets foot outside her own threshold, Eltifa had ample opportunities for matchmaking. Her blindness, of course, qualified her to be a musician. (For the life of us, Beatrice and I could see no logic in this statement, and Kalipha was obliged to explain that the sightless women of Kairouan are organized into little bands of minstrels that are hired on occasions of rejoicing in the hareems. It needs no special talent for singing to be an *Alimeh*, or professional singer. Any woman, so long as she is blind, is eligible, providing she can beg, borrow, or buy a drum and will set herself to learn the traditional songs. The orchestra to which Eltifa belonged was the foremost in Kairouan. They were so popular, indeed, by reason of the variety of their instruments and the extent of their repertory, that in festive seasons they could not fill their engagements and, even in dull times, they performed four nights out of seven.) 'She did her best, my poor sister,' Kalipha sighed. 'But the perfidy of those that have a *divorcée* on their hands! According to the uncle of—' he nodded significantly toward the court, 'she was everything that was practical! With food she was a magician, she would keep the house clean like sand, our raiment she would wash and mend, she was an expert, too, at the loom and would earn for me, over and over again, the price I paid for her. Moreover she had the energy of a tigress and the disposition of an angel!' He shook his head, laughing ruefully, 'She is, instead, an infliction of destiny! But what can one do? The fate of every man is inscribed on his forehead; all is written, or, as we others say, *mektoub!*'

'It is true,' Mohammed agreed with a hearty sigh, 'my father has no luck!'

During the evening the little boy was sent to invite his aunt and uncle to join us. Abdallah came first, bearing a tray of jiggling glasses and a small blue tea-pot. His face had the colour of a coffee bean, his eyes the brightness of jewels. Kalipha addressed him with evident respect and Fatma, after he had seated himself comfortably, set a fresh fire-pot before him. Mohammed returned with his hand on the arm of a large heavy woman, dressed like her sister-in-law, in jersey, vests, and trousers. Even before she reached the threshold she called us by name, greeting us with such heartiness, and laughing so at our exclamations of pleased surprise, that we were prepared to love Eltifa before we laid eyes on her. Her sightless face was fine and strong, full of gentleness and good humour. Still chuckling, she seated herself ponderously by the side of her little brown husband. I remarked upon the cheer and warmth that seemed to come in with her. Kalipha threw out his arms, 'My sister *illumines* the room!' It was easy to see that the whole family doted on her. Even Fatma took a place close beside her and, when we attempted to talk with her through Kalipha, she hid her smiling face in Eltifa's soft shoulder.

Abdallah's quiet hands moved among the tea things. Kalipha lit his kif-pipe and passed it to my friend. After a few puffs apiece they relapsed into dreamy silence. Beatrice, stretched full length upon the bed, her head pedestalled upon her hand, was completely relaxed. 'What do you see?' My question brought Kalipha back from Baghdad. 'The walls are magnificent with blue faience. All that,' he pointed to the crude beams above, 'is cedarwood carved in scrolls and rosettes, as delicate as lace. The room has enlarged to a vast *salon* spread with prayer-rugs and silken cushions. Someone unseen is playing the lute.'

The tea was ready. Abdallah was filling the little glasses with the ruby fluid. Then from a paper cone he poured a few roasted chick-peas, or *humsah*, into each glass and handed it out with a *'Saha!'* To thy refreshment! *'Yatikasaha!'* And to thine! We acknowledged the courtesy from a deep content. Eltifa produced her distaff and while she led the yarn from the shining fleece, Mohammed and the women talked together. Abdallah, the calm, took an occasional pinch of snuff from a large coloured handkerchief; now and then, as he listened his face shone with animation and he added a remark that filled the little room with quiet mirth.

'There is a story,' said Kalipha, tipping the tumbler for the tea-soaked pellets at the bottom, 'there is a story of *humsah* that has grown with Kairouan.' He shook the little glass and failing to dislodge the peas, he broke up the fraternity with a finger, tipped the glass once more and crunched meditatively. We waited patiently, sipping the bitter-sweet infusion for which Abdallah was justly renowned. Kalipha wiped his mouth with his handkerchief, smoothed his moustaches, straightened his shoulders and began, 'In former times there lived in this City a good man known by the name of Sidi Bohumsah.' Kalipha's face and gestures told the story as vividly as his tongue, so that Abdallah and the women who knew the tale, but no word of French, were able to follow it with as much relish as we. Hour after hour we listened, until Mohammed and Fatma slept in their places, and Abdallah and Eltifa finally took themselves off to bed. At one moment Kalipha was the canny wag who carried his whole fortune, a single *humsah*, under his tongue, the next moment he had puffed himself to a semblance of the sultan, and with equal ease and conviction so help me, he was Yesmeena, the sultan's daughter!

The night was far gone by the time Bohumsah, on the strength of a mythical fortune, symbolized by the chick-pea, discarded his shabby gown for a robe of honour that glistened with thousands of tiny mirrors, and, having become possessed of vast estates, and ships, and merchandise, he married Yesmeena with whom he lived in joy and prosperity 'until they were visited by the devastator of palaces and the replenisher of graves.'

DIFFICULTIES AND
ADJUSTMENTS

Kalipha became my constant companion in the days that followed. So ravenous was I for experience, and so indefatigable was he, that I had filled my note-books in no time. I read them over now with amusement. They were written in such excitement, voluminous surface accounts of marriage rites, camel battles, divorce courts, dancing dervishes, street and market scenes, fête days and parties! Beatrice seldom shared these experiences. Both Kalipha and I recognized her need to be left alone. It was a really gala occasion when she would join us of an evening.

Kalipha regarded me, therefore, as his especial protégée. We made the tour of his great family, all of whom hailed me as 'Sherifa,' the name Eltifa had given me after I had become a frequent visitor of the household. I went regularly with the women to the baths, often Eltifa and her sister musicians took me along with them to celebrations in various parts of the town.

When Kalipha's friends invited me 'to honour their houses,' he resigned his charge to Mohammed who was still young enough to have access to the hareems. Paying calls was no duty for Mohammed. Our pidgin French had given the little boy a funny dexterity in expressing himself and he was exceedingly proud to fill his father's shoes as my interpreter. He was a great favourite with the ladies wherever he went, enlivening their confinement like an animated courier on town events. Then, too, such visits, no matter how casual or unexpected, always meant food—sherbet, sweet cakes, or fruit-paste. Often, for want of such delicacies, the evening meal was brought forth in the great wooden bowl or *kassar*. I was sufficiently instructed in Arab etiquette, by this time, to know that we must never decline anything that is served. I was less sure, however, just how much we were expected to eat, and Mohammed's appetite used to appal me. 'Not so *much!*' I would murmur as the hole in his side of the bowl enlarged and deepened. For the next few moments he would eat sedately as it were, from the end of his spoon, but the women never failed to route his restraint with such vociferous encouragement that my concern for their husbands' supper often outweighed my own enjoyment.

Kalipha was not content that I should know only the manners and customs of his people, I must know the religion. My sincere interest in his form of worship led him to undertake my conversion. I had no wish to be a hypocrite. I tried my best to explain that, although I did want to know his Faith, I had no intention of embracing it. 'Ah, my little one, how can you know this?' he would expostulate. 'You are by nature, a Moslem,whether you know it or not. Allah works what He willeth. In your ignorance, you think it a mere accident that you came to this holy city. It is my belief, it was divinely ordained that you should come to Kairouan; it was ordained that we should meet so that, by my efforts, you can be numbered among the Faithful.'

The first thing he taught me, to this end, was the Call to Prayer, the *Adan*, that comprises the two grand principles of El-Islam. God is God, and Mohammed is His prophet! With what zeal and persistence he drilled me in that venerable chant! To recite the words was not enough, I had to practise—long after I was weary—until I could match the measure, the timbre, every last lingering cadence of the exhortation. His pride in my performance was inordinate. In the shops of his friends, in the homes of his relations, he would get me to give the *Adan*. It always evoked a burst of incredulous delight, Kalipha was vigorously commended, I congratulated and godspeeded upon my reformation. With what patience, too, he instructed me in his beliefs about djinns, both good and evil, about paradise, hell-fire, and the angels of death who would cause me to sit up in my fresh grave for the dread examination!

Sometimes he varied his instruction and taught me popular songs. They were love-sick plaints, for the most part, often, I surmise, a little lewd, sung to beautiful minor melodies. I, in turn, taught Kalipha, 'Lavender's blue, Dilly-dilly! Lavender's green! When I'm a king, Dilly-dilly, you shall be queen! Who told you so, Dilly-dilly? Who told you so? 'Twas mine own heart, Dilly-dilly, that told me so!' I tried out other tunes on him, but for rollicking rhyme and rhythm Dilly-dilly was the song for him! On our walks outside the ramparts in the early darkness he would march along bawling it at the top of his voice until it seemed that bedouins far out upon the plain must hear the noise with wonder.

I was spending very little time these days in the French town, but quite enough to be aware of its disapprobation. It was apparently a civic duty to warn us against the pariah, Kalipha ben Kassem. We ignored the hints and insinuations, but when it was seen that these didn't take, we were forced to hear the story of Kalipha's brother over and over again. 'Perhaps you do not know that this companion of yours is the brother of an assassin?' 'Yes, we have heard so, Monsieur.' This reply was always a surprise, making it somewhat awkward to proceed. When we asked why they would have us condemn the man for something his brother had done, the answer never varied, 'But he is the brother of an assassin, *quoi!* It goes without saying that he, himself, is a dangerous character! It looks very bad for you young women to associate with him.' That we continued to do so, did not ingratiate us with the French who decided that we were obviously no better than we should be.

The hotel, in the meantime, had become intolerable. We were paying far too much, the food was uncleanly, cockroaches came up from the kitchen, Beatrice's room was overrun with mice that made nightly feasts of her sketches, on top of which she had bedbugs! In all fairness to my friend, inasmuch as it will be remembered that she had prepared me, it must be explained that, ordinarily, she didn't mind bed-bugs. In fact her scale of living in Europe had more or less accustomed her to them. If it had been only bed-bugs! As it was, every day new disturbances made it more impossible for her to work and on the morning that she discovered her bed was infested, Beatrice took to the warpath.

Madame was horribly affronted, flatly refusing to believe that there were 'beasts' in a bed that had never been complained of before. She said she could sooner believe it of mine! To humour us, however, she sent the boy up to 'look it over.' On several occasions, after particularly hot rows, the mattress disappeared, presumably for renovation. We were never quite clear what happened to it between the time it was carried off on Hadi's head and sundown, when it was borne back again, but certain it was that, after each outing, the bugs thrived with new vigour. No satisfaction could be got from Madame; constant quarrels and complaints had driven her to drink and when she wasn't 'sick,' she was as elusive as a minnow. Beatrice, in angry despair, was on the point of leaving Kairouan.

Kalipha was all for moving us into the Arab town. The poor fellow was about crazy trying to stay my companion until he could find us other lodgings. But an apartment was not the answer. The expense of furnishing it, with even the necessities, would have left us nothing to live on. The alternative was an Arab hotel overlooking the great double gate that led to the market-place. This rheumy little joint, wedged among coffee-houses and open shops, did not exactly strike us as a place to run from vermin. Nevertheless it was, if it were to take Kalipha's word for it. Bed-bugs, he insisted scornfully, were strictly French. He 'guaranteed' that there would be none in the Arab hotel. He had already started negotiations with his friend, Sidi Tahar, the patron who, we were told, had invited us to give his beds several nights' trial that we might judge for ourselves. The least we could do, after that, was to inspect the place.

Its name, the Hôtel de Sfax, was a naive conceit. Strictly speaking, it was a caravanserai, patronized only by bedouins. Entering the street door, we climbed a narrow flight of stone stairs to a tiled, rather lofty corridor off which were seven whitewashed cells, each complete with an iron bed. Five of them were as dark and small as closets with only a transom for air, the end rooms were bigger and had windows that faced the tumultuous street. The front room was fairly spacious, in fact, and got a north light; the back one, which would be mine if we moved, overlooked a low white terrace, the roof of the coffee-house below.

In a last effort to convince the patronne of our so-called hotel that something had to be done, Beatrice made a collection of bed-bugs. She put all she caught in a saucer and one night she went down to supper ahead of time taking along her exhibit, prepared to have it out with Madame, drunk or sober. After waiting around the lobby for almost an hour—I having arrived in the meantime—she finally went in to eat. We were in the middle of the meal when, glancing towards the door, I was startled to see Madame, blowsy from her long binge, heading straight for our table. Crimson with fury, she trained her guns on Beatrice. We stared at each other, dumbfounded by this volley of noisy abuse. Suddenly the blank astonishment on my friend's face faded and she resumed her dinner, her shoulders shaking with laughter. She had, unintentionally, left the bed-bugs on the reception desk! Unaware of the incident, I was mystified, as much by her mirth as by this unwarranted harangue. 'I tell you, Mademoiselle, this woman is *méchante*.' I was asked to figure, if I pleased, what arriving guests would have thought to find those beasts on the registry. Fortunately, she had discovered the villainy before the train arrived. But, *mon dieu*, was an honest woman forced to support such wickedness? No, she assured me, she was not! She would make out our bills in the morning.

'You can make them out right now,' said Beatrice with a broad smile. It was days since she had felt so good!

Never was a move accomplished with more expedition, nor with such satisfaction so far as Kalipha was concerned. His delight in Beatrice's *faux pas* was shameless. He retailed it right and left. Everybody thought it hilariously funny. (For a joke on the French has a very special kick for the Arabs.) By the murky light of a candle-end our luggage was piled in the hall of the Hôtel de Sfax. 'Lavender's blue, Dilly-dilly! Lavender's green!' roared Kalipha superintending the proceedings. Ali, the door-keeper, the patron's younger brother, shuffled about, his big brown face glistening. He was a perfectly huge fellow in a bulbous pink turban. 'In Allah's name, be welcome!' he kept assuring us. There were no sheets to the beds, no towels, washbasins, lamps, not even a nail on which to hang anything, but we had Kalipha's promise that all our wants would be supplied on the morrow. None of us had a care that night!

Fortunately for our need to celebrate, Eltifa was entertaining her sister musicians, and the double household was ablaze with light and revelry. The insistent beat of the tom-toms, the ululant songs had brought neighbour women running across the roofs, their kerchiefed heads formed a bright frieze all around the parapet. Whenever the music slackened, they encouraged the festivities below with the *zaghareet*, shrill cries that fluttered off into the night air like the signal summons of the valkyrie. At 2 a.m. when we left, surfeited with tea, coffee, and fête cakes, worn out with the excitement of the drums, Eltifa's party had just begun.

The next day we made the acquaintance of our patron. Kalipha had instilled in us a very warm feeling for Sidi Tahar. We didn't entirely believe that he had been quite so inflamed when Kalipha described for him the filth of the hotel, or that he had vowed, should we consent to be his guests, he would move the Grand Mosque if it would add to our comfort. We were even sceptical as to whether he had really tendered us such flowery respects. Nevertheless, we felt warm towards him.

Besides the Hôtel de Sfax and the little restaurant beneath it, Sidi

Tahar was proprietor of a similar hostelry near the entrance to the *souks*. His headquarters were here. He sat cross-legged upon a high counter in the room at the head of the stairs. Serene, composed, with thin fine features— the face of an aesthete—he looked anything but a man of business. He welcomed us mildly, with a scarcely perceptible smile, and ordered chairs and coffee. Kalipha, in the meantime, seated himself genially upon the counter. The contrast between these two was something of a shock. Sidi Tahar had the bony delicacy of a high priest or an Arab grandee; his white turban was perched on the back of his head, his long hands moved gracefully out from the folds of his immaculate garments. Beside this high-bred canine Kalipha was an alley mutt, and for one moment, it seemed a little wonderful to me that I had so overcome my repulsion as to be only aware of the goodness in that swarthy hirsute visage.

There ensued, while we all sipped our coffee, an elaborate interchange of greetings and interminable inquiries concerning their respective households. In Arab business transactions the idea is to avoid brass tacks for as long as possible; we were never quite sure when they got down to them. Beatrice and I sat helplessly by as the leisurely conversation unrolled above us. Kalipha with oily smiles and tempered gestures was doing most of the talking, Tahar's face taking on not the slightest expression from which we could gauge the drift of the colloquy. Strain as we would for a familiar word, we could make nothing of this impenetrable thicket of gutturals. We were on our second round of coffees when Kalipha shiningly announced to us that the price had been agreed upon. One hundred francs, each, would cover our rooms, as well as our dinner, which was to be sent up from the restaurant each evening in covered casseroles. Room and board for four dollars a month was something like it! But now, what about clean sheets regularly, a table for me, lamps instead of candles, wash-stands, equipped with bowl and pitcher, a few hooks, and for each of us a towel? 'Be patient,' soothed Kalipha, 'we have not finished.' The thicket closed again and while the morning wore on Kalipha expounded our case. It seemed as if he must be apologizing for our fastidious requirements. (The regular clients, after all, have need of no more than a bed.) We caught the words *Amerique*, and *bahee yessir*, 'very delicate.' His gestures had become brief, attenuated, as if he were describing a pair of bijoux. But from neither Kalipha's unctuous affability nor Tahar's courteous attendance, his occasional bland comment, could we judge how far we had progressed, or if, indeed, we had progressed at all! From the full stops now, during which the two smoked thoughtfully, we sensed a deadlock. Kalipha's fez, which sometimes served as a sort of index to baffling situations, sat dispirited on the back of his head. Then he was speaking again and my jaded ears pricked up at the familiar sounds *Adan*, *kief-kief bellaraby*, 'exactly like a Moslem.' Tahar was looking at me, his eyes kind with interest, Kalipha like a proud parent about to show off the precocity of an offspring. 'Come now,' he chirruped, 'the *Adan*, and mind the long pause after *Akbar*.' Beatrice revived and regarded me with humour. She had never heard my *Adan* and I felt very foolish. 'Go on,' she encouraged, 'we forgot to say that we each need a chair.'

Kalipha had raised his hand like a baton, his mouth opened anticipatively. '*Allah akbar!*' I began, self-consciously. 'Wait!' interrupted Kalipha, scowling. 'Begin again! Louder, more clear! The voice of the *muezzin*, remember, must carry to the street. There is nothing in this chant, I believe, to make you ashamed! Hold your head up!'

'*Allah akbar! Ashed wullah elehheh ullala, ou ashed weneh Mohammed errusool Allah! Allah akba ! Haya alla Salat! Haya alla falah! Al-lah Akbar!*' I could see by his face that I had done Kalipha credit. Sidi Tahar was positively beaming. The first sibilant note had brought his half-brothers rather dazzled to the door. Kalipha, dull red with pleasure, was a study in righteous piety as their encomiums rained upon him. After that, all our wants were accorded us! We were even emboldened to ask for, and were graciously granted, the two chairs. Our business settled, more coffees were pressed upon us, Tahar gravely expressed through Kalipha, his hope that we would frequently honour his household, and a date was set for our first visit.

Beatrice was determined that we should waste no more than a day in getting settled. But we had yet to learn that nothing is so urgent to an Arab that it cannot be put off until tomorrow. The items we had asked for came piecemeal, with unconscionable waits between. The sheets, when they finally showed up, beautifully folded, bore the clearest evidence of having been slept on for weeks since last they were laundered. Ali, who was something of a dunce, finally admitted that they *were* pretty dirty, but, he was quick to assure us, they had come from the bed of the patron himself!

We had thought it would be such fun to have our dinner brought to us each evening like a surprise package. Kalipha's memorable meal had given us a relish for Arab food, or so we thought until we took the covers from two dubious-looking messes. One was a soup with a strong taste of rancid oil, and even Beatrice, who wasn't at all squeamish about food, baulked at the stew. Kalipha was on hand to see how we fared that first evening. He found us at my table eating oranges, the supper untouched beside us. He tasted each dish and, without a word, he threw them both in the slop-pail, and banged himself out of the room. We heard him raising an awful row in the restaurant below. He returned with Mohammed a few minutes later and laid out for us a full meal subtracted from their own supper. *Cous-cous* with camel meat, carrots and pumpkin, a cluster of dates which they had bought on the way, and chunks of Eltifa's crusty brown bread, still warm from the baking. And so, Kalipha appointed himself our chef, as he had already installed himself our 'cicerone, guide, guard, and historiographic squire.'

The Hôtel de Sfax had still other disadvantages, quite unforeseen. Beatrice's north light proved an ever-changing dazzle caused by the reflection of the glare against the chalk-white mosque opposite. Also, her room was right on top of the clamour and din of the street. It was like trying to concentrate in a boiler factory, while I almost suffocated at night. Because of the terrace outside my window, Kalipha insisted that I keep my shutters locked until daybreak, it was weeks before he could bestir them to put me behind bars. But there could be no compromise with the broken lock on my door. Kalipha was dynamite till *that* was fixed. He would tolerate neither excuse nor delay, in a towering rage he threatened to sleep outside my door. The locksmith arrived with unheard of alacrity! In short, without Kalipha, who was our advocate with Sidi Tahar, who bulldozed Ali, who argued, fought, soft-soaped, lied and swore for us, living in the Hôtel de Sfax would not have been possible.

My faith in our friend received a bad jolt, however, the day I discovered a bed-bug. Sanguine specks on the sheets had aroused suspicions which I had allayed by calling to mind his vehement 'guarantee.' Then I found that bug on the counterpane. I impinged it on a needle and showed it reproachfully to Kalipha. He shrugged his shoulders. 'But you find them everywhere!' he protested. Even Beatrice, considering her past attitude, was mighty complacent. 'Why, it stands to reason these beds are alive with bugs,' she said quite casually. So we let it go at that.

But, for all its shortcomings, we had found our place in Kairouan. Although she never admitted it, Beatrice was accustoming herself to the infernal racket. She found it no longer necessary to forage the crowded streets, she could sketch from her windows, or from the broad terrace that hung just above the heads of the throng.

At 7.30 each morning Salah, the kindly *cafetier* from across the street, brought us coffee. Beatrice and I seldom saw each other till evening, when she came into my room for dinner. (My room-since I had the table.) Shortly after the *muezzins'* call, the door was knocked and either Kalipha or Mohammed brought in the basket. Those little dinners—piping hot, perfectly prepared, eaten together in the cosy lamplight—are good to remember! We had finished and opened our books when Kalipha would appear with a firepot and the paraphernalia for tea. If we felt like talking, very good, but if we wanted to read, undisturbed, somehow he knew it without being told. He quietly kept the tea going and, curled up compactly on the bed, he smoked with a serenity that permitted us to forget all about him.

The French town had ceased to exist for us until the morning we received official notice that we were to appear that day before the *commissaire de police*. We had already submitted our passports, they were on file at the station; we had taken out our cards of identity, consequently we were puzzled by the rather peremptory summons.

In the absence of the Commissaire himself Monsieur S—, his assistant, received us. We knew at once that he had been drinking, and after he had put to us a few pointed questions his purpose, too, was apparent. We were here to be admonished on account of Kalipha.

'They tell me that you have taken up with this vagabond Courage.' The nickname which so characterized our friend, and conveyed in the Arab town such affection, had suddenly become insulting, opprobrious.

'Yes,' Beatrice replied, after a pause, 'it is true that we know Sidi Kalipha.'

This reply infuriated our inquisitor. '"*Sidi* Kalipha," *hein*?' he mocked her respectful use of the prefix, 'you call that miscreant "*Sidi*"?' He began to roar at us. With the violence of his passion, his face, red to begin with, took on the look of raw liver. We sat speechless. I was frightened, but Beatrice's eyes were blazing, she was gripping the arms of her chair. I started to explain our attitude towards our companion, but I was shouted scurrilously down. Beatrice got to her feet. 'Come on. Don't be a fool. You can't talk to him, he's drunk.' With his raucous voice still in our ears we made our way to the street.

We were cooling off in the market-place when Kalipha strolled up. He knew that we had been to the police-station, and he had a fair idea why. The declining sun filtered through the soft streamers of the pepper trees. Abashed, he took a seat beside us. Beatrice ordered him a coffee, and for a few minutes we all smoked in moody silence. 'Well?' he said at last, searching our faces. I reached over and found his hand. 'You look like a bridegroom!' Beatrice told him, smiling. She adjusted the little bunch of jasmine that hung over his ear, and studied him critically. Then, 'Can we get to work on that portrait the first thing to-morrow morning?'

A DJINN PARTY

We did not live among the Arabs for a month without learning something of djinns, nor without coming to feel a certain respect for phantoms that exert such influence over the learned and ignorant alike. Kalipha, who could not read or write his own name, believed implicitly in them, but so did young Ramah, a graduate of the Sorbonne, so did our merchant friend, Mohammed el Mishri, who made annual trips to the Continent. To acknowledge the Koran, in short, is to admit 'the might, majesty, dominion, and power' of djinns.

Before Adam even, they existed. Because they were created of 'smokeless fire,' they are extremely volatile, assuming any of a thousand guises and capable of becoming visible or invisible at will. Hosts of them in ages past were converted and, as True Believers, they now perform the prayers, give alms, fast during the sacred month of Ramadan, and make the Pilgrimage. These, the good djinns, visit men only to comfort and protect them, but beyond Kalipha's assertion that they certainly *did* exist, I heard very little of them.

It is the infidels, the *sheytan*, that abound in wickedness, inspiring a vigilance that is warp and woof of daily existence. You durst not empty a basin of water without uttering the magic word, craving pardon of the invisible one you may have soaked; to light the fire or let the bucket down into the well without 'Permission, ye Blessed!' is enough to throw consternation into an entire family; while to enter an uninhabited house, the baths, the public ovens, and, especially, the toilet, without a conjuration is tantamount to disaster.

Mohammed and Kalipha never mounted the staircase of the Hôtel de Sfax after dark without a prudent *'Bishmella! In the name of Allah!'* One night when Mohammed was accompanying me home he confided his fear that a djinn—maybe Iblees himself—was haunting the place. Hamuda, our coffee-boy, had been the first to suspect its presence. On three successive occasions, as he was ascending to serve us, he had fallen and broken the cups. The first two times his father had beaten him, but when it happened the third time 'they knew it was a djinn.' Mohammed swore that Ali, too, had heard curious, unaccountable noises in the corridor. My attempts at reassurance were powerless to rid him of the obsession. Unluckily, when we were climbing the stairs, he trod on his blouse. His fist shot above his head as he cried, 'What did I tell you!' Pride would not permit him to ask me to light his way down again, but a new link to the bond between us was forged when I held the lamp until he reached the street.

Kalipha saw nothing remarkable in the fact that most of the malice of djinns is perpetrated upon women. Their instability and weakness, indisputable even among themselves, makes them as clay in the hands of the evil ones. When woman was created, and from a crooked rib, at that, did not Iblees, the chief of the *sheytan*, send up the shout: 'Thou shalt be my arrow with which I shoot and miss not!' Man's very nature, supplemented, of course, by the seal ring upon his finger, protects him. But even he is by no means impervious. For example, there was a man in the town, a man of pious habits and exemplary character, who one day disappeared from the face of the earth. Nobody saw him leave, nobody knew why he left—least of all his wife and grown children. Friends and relatives joined the search. After a year had elapsed, with still no word from him, they divined the mystery. A djinneyeh had married him and spirited him to the underworld. In her good time he would return. Sure enough he did, at the end of two years. He appeared as he had vanished. It was said that when his wife, who was alone in the court at the time, saw him standing there she had a kind of fit. Kairouan could talk of nothing but Sidi Woomah's homecoming. But he himself was strangely taciturn. In answer to the eager questions with which he was besieged, Woomah would lay a finger upon his lips, and the most that could be got from him was an enigmatic, 'One does not speak of this.' Gradually, however, as evening after evening he sat with his friends in the coffee-house, it became less difficult for him to speak of his experience. It had been, by all the accounts I heard, anything but unpleasant. The djinns, perhaps to make him feel more at home, had worn the aspect of humans and had treated him with great politeness. The climate of the nether world, too, had been unvaryingly balmy. Nobody dreamed of questioning Woomah's credibility, though I think it did surprise them to hear that there had been 'automobiles, gendarmes, and all sorts of machinery.'

It was all very puzzling to me because, although the djinns had stolen Sidi Woomah, which was certainly not praiseworthy of them, they did not sound like a really bad lot. 'Were they wicked djinns ' I asked Kalipha.

'N-o-o-o,' he said, thoughtfully shaking his head.

'They were good ones, then?'

'They were like us,' he replied, 'good ones and bad ones, with a little good in the bad ones and some bad in the good ones.' A trifle exasperated, I recklessly suggested that Woomah might have voluntarily dropped out of sight, maybe because of ennui (if his wife was subject to fits), maybe wanderlust. It sounded to me, I said, as if he'd been having one fine time down in Biskra or Touggourte!

Under Kalipha's steady gaze I felt my colour rise and I repented of my heresy. 'Nobody,' he declared gravely, 'not even the *bash mufti* himself is more devout than Sidi Woomah.' Wagging his finger he proceeded to rebuke me with this proverb: '"If you hear that a mountain has moved from its place, believe it, but if you hear that a man has changed his character, do not believe it, for he will act only according to his nature."'

The few times I saw Sidi Woomah he was surrounded with men whose faces wore the fixed look of children hearing a ghost story. He had not been home much over a year, however, when it was voiced about town, 'Have you heard? Sidi Woomah is not to be found!' The wise smiles with which this intelligence was given and received made me surmise that his lot might be considered a very enviable one, but I never intimated my suspicion to Kalipha, feeling sure that he would be obliged to deny that such a fate was anything but deplorable.

Close association with Kalipha's household meant a very practical schooling in demonology. Whenever Abdallah left the family circle of an evening it was because the wife or daughter of so-and-so was possessed, and at least two-thirds of Eltifa's engagements were *fokkarahs*, or parties for the propitiation of some woman's djinn.

The djinn, it seems, enters the body by way of the brain and searches until he finds a place to lodge. He announces his seizure with unmistakable symptoms—loss of appetite, listlessness, fits of yawning or bad temper. A practised seer like Abdallah is sent for, and, with chaplet and holy writ, he makes a formal investigation. The patient and her family gather in a dark room. Abdallah sits facing them, chanting the Koran and rhythmically swaying, now and then dropping another lump of *benjoin* upon the fire-pot. Lulled by the fumes of the djinns' favourite incense, the family rock with him, intoning the familiar passages. Often it is a long time before the spirit responds and the woman begins to jabber. She goes through the progressive stages of the trance until the djinn is rampant, causing her to rave and foam at the mouth. Now Abdallah can converse with the guest. With the utmost civility he is made welcome. Then the question is put to him, 'What is it ye crave, O ye Blessed?' and the patient's lips articulate the djinn's response. 'A reading of the Koran will content me,' he may say, or, 'For the love of Araby, Sidi, kill a lamb that I may drink the blood!' Generally, however, he wants a *fokkarah*, in which case a night is set, the woman's friends are invited, and the musicians engaged to play upon the *bangha*, a powerful Congo drum, the beat of which makes the demon well-nigh delirious with delight. To the pounding of the *bangha* the patient dances, sometimes for hours, until her djinn is appeased and she drops in a swoon. The guests work over her then, chanting exorcisms as they systematically pull her nose, ears, toes and fingers. The djinn may leave, *but he may not*.

If, in a few days, the symptoms repeat themselves, Abdallah makes another visit. Sometimes the tormentor can be bribed with delicacies—a diet of raw meat and eggs, or the blood of a black chicken. But when persuasive measures are unsuccessful a scroll, penned with certain verses from the Koran, is burned and the patient inhales the smoke—none but the most tenacious *sheytan* can withstand this dreadful vapour! If even this fails to evict him, Abdallah is justified in announcing that the djinn has married his patient. So a compact is made with him. If he elects to remain where he is, he must agree to be quiescent until the anniversary of his seizure. If he leaves his bride, he must not return until that date. In both cases he will be made festally welcome. To 'tie' the djinn to his promise Abdallah makes his patient an amulet—a bit of the Koran encased in leather or velvet—which she pins among her garments or on her headkerchief.

As I understand it, it is only when the sprite settles in the *brain* itself that his victim succumbs. Be this as it may, most of the women that died while I was living in Kairouan were taken of djinns. When death. occurs criers from the mosques broadcast the obituary through every quarter of the city. 'Hark!' Kalipha would say at sound of that sombre chant ; then, when he had gathered its purport, he would sigh: 'There is no strength or power but in Allah! Sidi Bombourt's daughter, a girl of fifteen, has just died of a djinn.' Another sigh and he would add laconically : 'This afternoon she leaves her father's dwelling without the veil.'

There were many things about djinns that perplexed me. Why, for instance, when given the choice of various forms of entertainment, did they generally demand the *fokkarah*? Kalipha accounted for this with a hunch of the shoulders. 'It's a matter of taste, that's all. You like chicken, I prefer lamb. It is the same with the djinns.' Altogether, as my mentor on this subject, Kalipha was about as inchoate as I would have been had I attempted to explain for his complete satisfaction the holy trinity. *'Tiens,'* he said, perceiving that his answer left me still in doubt, 'the next time there is a *fokkarah* in the family, you shall attend.'

We had not long to wait. The following week there was one at the home of his niece, Kadeja, a household almost as familiar to us by now as Kalipha's own. Kadeja was married to a bedouin, and though they made their home among his tribe far out upon the plain, they were spending this winter in Kairouan. It was Kadeja's neighbour, Shelbeia, who was giving the *fokkarah*. The same dwelling housed both families, who shared the common court, but Kadeja's apartment being the larger, was to be used for the occasion.

We hardly knew what to expect. It was the tenth anniversary of Shelbeia's spirit marriage, and, in accordance with the covenant, she must celebrate the bridegroom's return. This we understood, yet reasoned it must, of necessity, be quite a serious affair. We were as nervous as cats when we arrived at the house. Lighted windows and doorways illumined the court across which Kadeja hastened to greet us. We had never seen her dressed in such finery, her hands and wrists were dyed with henna, her brows and lashes blackened with kohl. She positively sparkled with gaiety and excitement. Boolowi, her little stepson, came running to meet us, and Sidi Farrah, her husband, towered smiling in the doorway.

The room, which may have been twice the size of Kalipha's, looked spacious to-night. The painted chest, the loom, and the kitchen utensils had been removed to the court and Kadeja's rug, cut from the frame only a few days ago, was spread upon the bed. In a row against the wall facing the door sat the black shrouded figures of the musicians. Kadeja's mood on the one hand and these sombre presences on the other created in us an even greater uncertainty as to the exact nature of the occasion. With restraint we acknowledged our welcome. We were composing ourselves upon the bed when one of the black bundles chirruped to us in Eltifa's voice, 'Welcome, O Rose! In Allah's name be welcome, O Sultana!' A standard feature of our evenings at Kalipha's was a little game in which each side made extravagant attempts to out-compliment the other. Eltifa's startling salutation solicited from us like rejoinders. 'Eltifa is like the jasmine,' we told her hesitantly, hardly daring to smile. 'Eltifa is the golden date.' Her sister performers came to her assistance now and it needed all Kalipha's ingenuity for Beatrice and me to hold our own in so unequal a contest. The vociferous merriment which it provoked relieved us of any further constraint.

Suddenly Shelbeia, bedizened with bright silks and party make-up, appeared on the threshold. It was something of a shock to find *her* in such high spirits! There was not the slightest indication that she housed a rampaging djinn. I appealed to Kalipha, 'Then this is not really such a serious occasion?' He seemed at loss for an answer.

'Serious, yes,' he replied, 'but not *too* serious.'

Shelbeia summoned the musicians to dinner and they filed out in lock-step murmuring and laughing among themselves. Kadeja then deposited the kassar before us and while Kalipha, Farrah, Beatrice and I devoted ourselves to the excellent macaroni, Boolowi, not yet of an age when he might eat with the men, sat patiently by in his high Egyptian fez. When the bowl was removed and the coffees were served, Kadeja and the little boy, their backs towards us, ate their own supper at the opposite end of the room.

Now and then as she turned her head I saw that Kadeja's profile was singularly pure. Smallpox had long ago cheated her of any claim to beauty, it was doubtful whether she could see from one eye, but the warmth of her character, her ripe personality endowed even her ravaged countenance with a kind of beauty. How different she was from the spineless neurotic women I had met and yet she had been conditioned to the same inviolable seclusion that had made them what they were. 'Ah, Kadeja. She is another thing,' was her uncle's way of putting it, 'she is like a man!'

The supper things had been cleared away when the thud of the knocker followed by Shelbeia's shrill melodious joy-cries sent Kadeja flying into the court. The guests had arrived. 'Alla-la-cen! Alla-la-cen!' Again and again the *zaghareet** pierced the confused greetings and solicitous inquiries. 'In Allah's name, be welcome!' 'How are you, my sister!' 'And Baba Mohammed?' 'Well, thanks be to Allah!' 'And Fatma?' 'And thy maternal grandmother?' 'May the occasion profit thee!' 'And the little ones?' 'Welcome in the name of Allah!' 'There is no ill?' 'To Allah be the praise!' During the flurry, Shelbeia's husband, a grave kindly fellow, slipped in and was invited to sit with us on the bed.

Chattering, laughing, unpinning their veils, ten or twelve women entered. Most of them, being old friends, doffed their *haïks* without shame before the three men, the exceptions remained cocooned, one in white, the other in black wrappings—a state which, as the evening progressed, appeared not to incommode them in the least.

From our vantage seat at the far end we watched the long narrow room transformed into a kaleidoscope of brilliant colours—rose, peacock blue, green, orange, cerise, gold and purple—shifting and glittering in the murky lamplight. Kalipha's other sister Jannat was there, a short, plump woman with the face of a clean little pig and we were pleased to see that Fatma had been allowed to come. She was already apart from the guests busying herself with preparations for tea looking as if she desired nothing so much as to be unobserved. The women made cushions of their *haïks* and produced from bodices and handkerchiefs their little hoards of toasted pumpkin seeds. While Fatma and Kadeja were passing the mint tea the musicians with their instruments crept back; Shelbeia leading the *chef d'orchestre*, the others tailing in lock-step. They seated themselves like witches in a ring, Kadeja placed before them a fresh fire-pot and they began beating the tom-toms and pottery drums, sounding them from time to time, a tuning up that added an anticipative tremor to the gaiety. Behind them stood a large authoritative drum, obviously the *bangha*. I

---

* This call of the women of Islam has no human sound to unaccustomed ears. It is the cry of a creature half-bird, half-woman—high, thin weird and shrill.

looked with wonder from it to the radiant Shelbeia, to her husband who seemed just as indifferent to the significance of the occasion.

A draped arm now held up a tambourine, gave it a warning shake. There was a brief silence. Then the minstrels let loose, bawling the songs of the day with novel variations of their own invention. The guests had to scream to make themselves heard and although shoulders had begun to ripple only the men seemed consciously listening. They reclined comfortably smoking, now and then a particularly hot passage evoking from one of them a gusty sigh, a groan of pleasure. At the first beat of the tom-toms Boolowi, close beside me, started to sway. At length, unable to bear it any longer, he stepped off the bed and began to undulate, his arms extended, one bare foot beating the rhythm. His chubby brown face was expressionless, his lids were lowered, the tall fez had toppled to one ear. In his comical absorption he was as unconscious of the mirth he provoked as if he were hypnotized. Assaulted with merry directions, he attempted first one movement, then another. Kadeja snatched off her pink *takritah* and twisted it about his waist. Boolowi beaming as he watched her nimble fingers. 'There, so! May Allah aid thee!' laughed Kadeja and he began again with new verve. Shelbeia, too, had started to dance. Four or five joined her, while the others clapped the metre.

It was an implacable sort of 'dance' for they simply stood, their arms rigid or dangling, their hennaed feet marking the time of the drum beats. The only variety was in the accompaniment. Faster or slower, it was always the same purposeful jig, no grace, no ardour, no sign of pleasure even when they were panting and prancing to keep up with the wild pounding of the drums. One of the performers was of such an enormous size it seemed that nothing short of a miracle could keep this party from becoming an *accouchement*.

Kalipha confirmed what we surmised: they were not dancing for the love of it, but for the good of their djinns. There is nothing, he said, like the tom-toms and particularly the *bangha* for rousing a dormant djinn, creating in him such a terrible yearning to dance as to make the best-intentioned forget his bargain. And if his protégée does not indulge him he will see that she pays for his disappointment.

'How! What will happen?'

'Headaches, rashes, boils, eye-trouble—if nothing worse. That woman *au gros ventre* does well to dance, for the djinn of a certainty would

45

destroy the child in her womb. But this is nothing,' Kalipha waved a belittling hand toward the surging figures. 'Presently you will see Aisha dance!' He pointed out an angular young woman in a lavender *takritah*. Her black hair hung in strings about her pale, sharp, almost gaunt face, a restive gipsy quality in her had fascinated us from the moment she had stepped into the room. Kalipha called to her and she glided over and crouched near the bed. Her face brightened when Kalipha told her that we hoped she would dance for us. *'Mleah,'* very good, she said, studying us curiously.

The musicians paused for rest and refreshment. They had no more than finished their tea, however, when they were tautening their drums. The intermittent thud of the *bangha*—ominous and hollow—warned that we were down to the real business of the evening. The women were compressing themselves in a radiant panel against the walls. Instinctively I searched for Shelbeia. Surely by now some sign would betray the heroine, but she was squeezed among the others laughing and gesticulating as if the *bangha* was for anybody's djinn but her own. The musicians fell upon their instruments with terrific force and fury. The clash-bang of tambours, the thud of tom-toms were almost lost beneath the accented beat of the jungle-drum. It seemed as if the walls could never contain the primordial booming! Kalipha must have passed the word around that Aisha was to dance, for every eye was upon her. She sat near us, her own eyes closed, her hands loose in her lap. I wanted to run from the abhorrent pounding as I watched her head and sinewy back weave the rhythm. All at once she leapt to her feet and slithered down the room, her magnificent body, lithe hips, long feet, angular arms, at one with the sensuous beat of the *bangha*. 'God' gasped Beatrice leaning forward, 'Good God!' The fire, the archaic beauty, the furious abandon! Wilder, more impassioned became her movements with the increasing violence of the beat. She shook her head free of the kerchief, her hair streamed about her rapt face, she tore off her jackets uttering shrill ecstatic cries, writhing and swaying until in a swoon she would have fallen if the women hadn't sprung out to grab her.

Simultaneously, the room was clamorous with confusion, the *bangha* stopped abruptly, Aisha was dumped in a corner and the noisy women were milling in and out of the court, cawing and bleating Shelbeia-Shelbeia-Shelbeia. I had a confused recollection of having seen a person in bright blue dart from the room toward the climax of the dance. The women, screaming like cormorants, were bringing something in. Beatrice and I rose upon our knees but the women had massed themselves about their burden. 'Don't be frightened,' smiled Kalipha. 'Hark!' he lifted a finger. It sounded as if someone was being strangled to death. '*C'est le djinn qui parle,*' he said casually, and we realized that, in spite of the hysteria, the women did not seem really alarmed, as for the men they smoked on, unconcernedly. 'But what happened?' we demanded.

'It is nothing. The *bangha* excited Shelbeia's djinn and she quit the room from a too great a desire to dance.' The frightful gasping and blubbering gradually subsided to tearful moans. 'Hear that djinn!' exclaimed Kalipha, whacking his thigh, '*comme il est furieux!*'

A few minutes more and Shelbeia, looking somewhat dazed, was stood upon her feet. For some, obscure reason, they threw a burnous over her shoulders and drew the great hood down over her face. The drums began again, more moderately, and the weird white cone, bowed with exhaustion, marked the time. Everybody, with the exception of Kadeja and Fatma, was dancing. The dusky room was a frenzy of agitated colours, the shimmer, flash and shine of bangles, tinselled braid and embroidery. Even the pair voluminously masked in their *haïks* bobbed away like truant spooks at a carnival. Boolowi had fallen asleep at last, literally on his feet, and was deposited behind us where he sat cross-legged, his eyes glued shut, gently rocking.

Aisha, who had recovered by this time, came of her own accord to sit alongside us. She was addressing Kalipha with such earnestness, glancing at us so meaningly that we waited with impatience for an interpretation. When she had done Kalipha heaved a deep sigh, 'Life is very difficult!' Aisha, unhappy with her husband, sick of her existence, had appealed for our help to get to America. I think Beatrice would have given a year of her life that night to be able to assist that gifted dancer. 'There is nothing you can do,' Kalipha admitted. 'But,' he added, 'I will not tell her that.' Aisha's famished eyes travelled from face to face as she waited for our answer. 'Leave it to me,' said Kalipha after a little thought, and before we realized what he meant, he was telling Aisha that Beatrice was resolved not to close her eyes that night until she had written to her relatives, all of whom had *barsha fluss*, he rubbed a thumb against his fingers suggestively. Aisha had only to bide the time with patience. Colour crept over her cheekbones, a wan smile flickered about her lips and she patted her chest with heart-rending gratitude. Kalipha turned to us complacently. 'Now she will hope for a time.' Beatrice was speechless with anger. I felt all the futility of railing against anything as subtle as Kalipha's code of honour, nevertheless I protested. 'She will know at last that she has been deceived. What then?'

'Ah, *then*,' he said, 'she will accept her fate. If it be the will of Allah that Aisha should go to America, my friend, *she will go to America*. How many times have I explained that if a man is destined to die on the land, he can be bound and thrown into the sea yet he will not drown, and if it is decreed that he shall be drowned, he will drown though he be cast upon a desert.'

Beatrice started to say something, instead she shrugged her shoulders with a 'Hell—what's the use!'

The hour was late, the air a smothering compound of smoke, incense, perfume, and body heat. Perspiring dancers, their hair leaping to the lurid boom-boom of the *bangha*, divested themselves of their outer garments. Shelbeia's hooded form still indefatigably footed it, like a heart that continues to throb long after life is extinct. Occasionally someone crumpled and was dragged to the sidelines where others were being revived or crouched apathetically until they were sufficiently recovered to start in again. Aisha pulled Kadeja to her feet insisting that they dance together. Kadeja laughingly protested, looking to her husband for permission. 'Let her! Let her!' shouted Kalipha for Farrah had given a grunt of disapproval. 'Ya Kadeja!' he barked above the hilarious laughter that applauded their version of the stomach-dance. Kalipha turned on him with anger and Farrah, his handsome face quite stern, relapsed into silence. Kadeja, taking no more notice of her husband, strode into the room in his street-robe, her *takritah* was bound turban-wise about her brow, her face blackened to resemble moustache and beard. Even Farrah's face relaxed at her gruff mimicry.

Apparently it struck neither of the men as inconsistent with Kalipha's behaviour that *his* wife had not danced all evening. I could not but feel that she must want to dance, that only a nod from her husband was needed to set her jogging. His genial smiles vanished as I offered the suggestion, though he affected not to hear me. 'Just this once,' I coaxed. 'What is good for Kadeja must be equally good for Fatma.'

'She cannot dance,' he hedged, Fatma's good being a matter of perfect indifference to him.

'Nonsense! Every Arab woman can dance.'

'She does not want to, then. Ask her if she doesn't prefer minding the tea.'

'There, she is looking this way! Make a sign to her!'

He shrugged impatiently, muttering, 'She has shame in dancing before her husband.'

'She does not dance because you will not trouble yourself to give her permission. If you—'

'Oh, let me alone!' he cried with an angry flounce.

The party would go on until daybreak, but by three o'clock Beatrice and I had had enough. Kalipha piloted us, drunk with fatigue, through the dark streets. Our little tiff—not the first of its kind—was bothering him. He did not venture to take my arm, but stumped along between us, his forehead knotted with gloom. I knew from experience that he would not bid me good night until things had been put right between us, and that he was pondering how best to go about it. Nothing was attempted, however, until he fitted the great key into the lock of the street-door. 'Tomorrow,' he said resolutely, 'I am going to buy Fatma a bag of those lozenges—you know, the square green kind, very strong with mint. It is true they are not cheap, but no matter! She is so fond of them. She will be pleased, won't she! Tell me, *ma petite*,' he beseeched, almost shyly, 'is this not a good idea?'

'A marvellous idea!' I agreed.

Completely reassured, Kalipha humped off down the silent street to the jocund strains of Dilly-dilly. And for the thousandth time since making his acquaintance, I reminded myself of Fielding's sage counsel: 'Let me admonish thee not to condemn a character as a bad one because it is not perfectly a good one.'

THE PASSING OF ZINIBE

K alipha could take or leave most of his women relations. He was perfectly content to be their mainstay in sickness, chief comforter in their sorrow, magistrate in any serious domestic difficulty and, once things were going smoothly again, to leave them strictly alone. The frequency of his visits since I had come to Kairouan was, therefore, immensely gratifying. They reproached him playfully when they told me: 'B'Araby, Sherifa, stay with us for ever because if you depart, it is unlikely that we will ever see him again!'

Although he was thus indifferent to most of the women in his family there were a few exceptions. He disliked his sister Jannat and never willingly went near her, while he detested Saida, her eldest daughter. Eltifa, the matriarch of the family since the death of his mother Mench, he loved and revered; Kadeja, also, was a favourite, and there could be no doubt that Zinibe shared with these two first place in his affections.

She was the only one of his nieces I had not met. Shortly after I came, Zinibe had fallen ill, and in the expectation that she would soon be better, our visit was postponed from week to week. It would pain her, Kalipha said, to be unable to receive her uncle's friend fittingly. It might do her even actual harm. I could not oppose such an argument.

'She is like a *bijou*,' he said, cupping and examining his hands as if they held her preciousness. 'Always laughing, always gay! Everybody's troubles are heavier than her own—*mon dieu*, she has a heart for all the world! And beautiful! You think my niece Fafanie beautiful. She is beautiful only until you have seen Zinibe!'

At my age, twenty-seven, Zinibe had six children, the oldest a boy of thirteen, and she had lost—to the best of Kalipha's recollection—at least three. On the subject of her talents Kalipha was exuberant. There was a taste to her cooking, 'A taste!' He kissed his finger-tips for want of any adequate description. I could have no conception of Arab hospitality until I had been entertained by Zinibe. Weaving, too, was her *forte*. Her loom was never vacant, as soon as one rug was cut down another was started, for she clothed the children with her own earnings. Kalipha had so little to say of Sallah, her husband who operated a barber shop on the marketplace, that I was quite ready to believe him blessed far beyond his deserts.

But management and thrift, the prime requisites of a good wife, were not the qualities that endeared her most to Kalipha. She was generous, loving, and gay. How the family would celebrate her recovery! 'I assure you,' he cried, 'it will be as if my niece were returned from the Pilgrimage. Another fortnight—by the grace of Allah!'

At last there came a time when Kalipha announced: 'This afternoon we are going to visit Zinibe.' Only the day before when I had asked about her he had answered: 'Man is like an ear of wheat shaken by the wind—sometimes up, sometimes down! We must have patience.'

In my surprise now I exclaimed: 'Then she is really better.' But Kalipha shook his head: 'Sallah has gone to fetch the *Roumi* doctor.' He had no need to say more. To seek the help of an unbeliever was an admission of desperation and defeat.

A little girl admitted us to the court. She looked about seven, she may even have been eight, but she had the grave sweet eyes of a woman. 'And how is Ummi?' asked Kalipha in a low voice.

'Praise be to Allah, the Lord of the universe,' Awisha said with a shrug and a pious glance at the sky.

'There is no strength nor power but in Allah, the high, the great,' murmured Kalipha as we followed her into the sick-room. A lamp burned uncertainly in the chamber-niche. Zinibe lay across the middle of the great bed and on either side of her sat the watchers. They greeted us with tearful grimaces, gestures of resignation, as they crowded closer, making place for us. Zinibe's dark cheeks were flushed, there was a frightened look in her large eyes. 'May Allah restore thee,' we told her. Zinibe spoke in little gasps, 'How are you, my uncle?' and to me: 'Welcome in the name of Allah.' Her voice was plaintive, like that of a child.

The room was crowded with her suffering and the august, overpowering presence of Allah. They were speaking of Him as 'merciful'

51

and 'compassionate,' but it was only flattery to stay His dreadful hand. Eltifa was weeping inaudibly. Fafanie's pretty face was so disfigured I hardly recognized her. Kadeja in her black robes opened her mouth only to sigh, her eyes were swollen and red. Zinibe's baby lay in the lap of her sister-in-law and whenever her mother-in-law, old Ummi Sallah, caught my eye she would point to the sleeping child and then to the ceiling, the tears trickling down her withered cheeks. But Zinibe's mother was not crying. Her face was as grey as stone. God knows what was passing through her mind as she sat, her arms around one knee or her hand upon her cheek. I was dumb, stupefied. There was absolutely nothing to say that would not have sounded empty, hypocritical. Words of hope or encouragement would have smothered under the weight of such anguish.

The lamp was held for us to see the bottle of medicine which the French doctor had left. Although Kalipha could not read, he feigned to study the label. He had something of a reputation in his family for medical knowledge, having served as apprentice to the French druggist for a short time in his youth. He put a few questions to his niece, then lifted her green gingham chemise and professionally probed her torso. The prints of his fingers on her bloated abdomen melted as if upon soft wax. '*Le mal c'est dans le rognon,*' he told me, '*il y a cinq jours qu'elle n'as pas pissé du tout.*' Zinibe was watching him. 'What is your opinion, my uncle? Have I a chance?' It was very difficult for her to speak. Casting up his eyes, Kalipha raised one finger and answered her with a single word 'Allah!' Zinibe made eager little sounds of agreement and she, too, held up a finger. '*Aywah!*' That is right! said her uncle approvingly, as he pulled the covers over her again. 'Allah has willed the recovery of sicker persons than you. Our sole help is in Him, the Mighty, the Merciful.'

There were gusts of agreement from the women. 'Praise be to Allah, Lord of the universe!' 'He aideth whom He will!' 'He is the First and the Last! There is no god but Allah!' Eltifa took the handkerchief from her eyes and said brokenly: 'No one can die except by His permission!'

'"According to the Book that fixeth the term of life."' Kalipha finished solemnly.

Two chubby little fellows in outgrown burnouses kept wandering in and out of the room. The knocker fell from time to time and Awisha would leave her place near her mother's dark head and run with a clinking of anklets to open the door. Each newcomer, after being shown the bottle of medicine, sat herself down to sigh among her wrappings. Just as we were about to go, the two oldest boys, Ali and Mohammed, came in from school. They glanced fearfully toward the bed and then, looking greatly relieved, greeted us with exquisite courtesy. Now Kalipha instructed me to repeat after him, word for word, a ceremonious parting speech. But that must not be. 'Just tell her,' I interrupted him eagerly, 'that when she is better I will come often—we will spend whole days together.' She turned soft eyes upon me and when Kalipha had finished she said, barely above a whisper: 'Come, and be sure of a welcome. May Allah cherish thee.'

I was eating my breakfast next morning when Kalipha came in. From the window he shouted to Hamuda for a cup of coffee and then sat down heavily and lit a cigarette. 'My niece died at six o'clock this morning,' he said as casually as if he were mentioning an incident of no great importance. 'The public mourner is at the house and the women are wailing and scratching their faces.' Somehow I had not thought that Zinibe would really die; I only half-believed that she was dead. Presently, I thought, he will tell me that it is all a mistake. Hamuda came in with the coffee. 'May Allah preserve the survivors!' he said.

Everybody knew, then, that Zinibe was dead, but I did not believe it, even though I cried, 'So young! And her children! What will become of them? Oh, Kalipha, why did it have to be Zinibe! Her mother, or old Ummi Sallah could so much better have been spared!' But Kalipha would not listen to such blasphemous talk. Did I presume to question the will of Allah?

Early that evening Kalipha, Mohammed and I went to the house to offer our respects. Kalipha left us at the door and repaired to a little mosque across the street where the men of the family were gathered. Sallah's sister Ummulkeer admitted us. She tried to acknowledge our condolences, but grief choking her, she gestured despairingly with the lamp. There was the buzz and drone of many voices, a soughing of unmistakable sorrow. The court was dark, save for the light that came from the windows, and eerily patterned with black and white draped figures. The room itself was jammed, gabbling with women. They sat three or four deep against the walls. The chamber-niche, which yesterday had been a sombre bed of pain, was a brightly lighted catafalque for the quiet body. It was wrapped in brilliant silk—long stripes of red and green—and the women were solidly banked on either side of it. No one seemed conscious that we had come in. We stood on the threshold looking for a place to sit down when Kadeja, catching sight of us, beckoned us to the bed where the relatives were seated. I did not see how there could be room for us, indeed I hoped there was not, but by crowding a space was made right alongside the corpse. I had never been so near one in my life.

In contrast to the vociferous grief of those on the floor, the women on the bed were composed, emotionally exhausted after a day of strenuous mourning. For, as soon as Zinibe had expelled her last breath, they had begun, and all morning they had danced, beating and clawing their faces in frantic grief. Their eyes were puffed and swollen, the faces of some of them were hideously scratched. Kadeja bared her arms to show me the livid welts that ran from her wrists to her shoulders.

Awisha drew the silken pall aside that we might view her mother's face. Yesterday I had seen only the vivid cheeks, the large frightened eyes, but fever and fear were gone now. Zinibe knew for a certainty what the rest must accept on faith. It was a lean sensitive face, luminous as amber in the lamplight. The cheek-bones were high, the arched brows and long lashes very black. So calm, so remote she looked. It was as if she would say: 'See, it is not difficult.' She had been conscious, they said, even when they turned her over toward the East and closed her eyes; she had given herself up like a child. The women fell to weeping at the sight of Zinibe's face and with a faint smile of pride the little girl covered it again, then settled herself, her hands in her lap, a deep bewilderment in her roving eyes.

Zinibe's mother, Ummi Kadusha, was not among the chief mourners on the bed. It was some time before I found her for she was off at the other end of the room. Her head was bowed, she sat with one leg under her, her hands clasping her knee. The women around her were all crying convulsively, as they rocked back and forth, combing their cheeks with their finger-nails. But the brooding figure stirred only to change her position.

Mohammed nudged me: 'Look, the *nahwehe!*' A middle-aged woman in white had come in from the court. She seated herself near the fire-pot, applied her knuckles to the tambour, and began a dolorous chant, half-wail, half-song, extolling the perfections of Zinibe. Not much of this was needed to set the women off. They broke into wild inconsolable weeping—shrieking, moaning, imploring Zinibe to get down from her bier. It seemed almost wonderful that she could sleep through such a din. After every few lines a violent paroxysm seized the *nahwehe* and she could not go on. The grief which had been gathering in her heart as she sang burst in a sob that shook her entire body. The women sobbed with her, an ancient wail of unutterable desolation. 'Who was so generous as she?' the *nahwehe* took up her cadenced lament, 'The beggars had a path worn to her door. *B'Araby*, she would take the food from her mouth to feed the hungry. Oh, the kindness of that heart! Alas, it beats no more! Ah-Ah-Ah!' The hopeless yearning of that cry was more than I could bear, my eyes flooded with tears. 'She must have loved Zinibe like a sister,' I said to Mohammed.

'What do you mean?' he sobbed. 'The *nahwehe* didn't know her.'

I realized with a start that I had been completely taken in, hoodwinked by the drama of it all. That very morning Kalipha had patiently explained the function and *modus operandi* of the public mourner. I was half-ashamed of my tears, the lump in my throat. This, after all, was her job. She did not have to know the deceased. In seven cases out of ten she had never laid eyes on her. But to the expert wailing woman this is no handicap. She knows all the secret springs of melancholy, she knows that the stricken will mourn the loss of qualities which the deceased did not possess. Thus she can generalize for hours and, by keeping one ear up, the cunning *nahwehe* can also particularize, and weave into her dirge specific instances of the dead woman's kindness and devotion.

After I had straightened things out in my mind, I became aware that there was a definite melody and measure to the throbs that had seemed so terribly sincere. They served as a chorus to each impromptu stanza, a conventional refrain in which the women joined her with apocryphal passion. If I had tears, therefore, let me shed them—for Zinibe's mother over there, or for little Awisha, who didn't understand that she was motherless.

At long intervals the *nahwehe* would let up and everybody would relax, almost thankfully, I thought. A rational sobriety would have begun to settle when she would start them up again. She was very business-like, almost too conscientious, in fact, for once, during a particularly long and harrowing recital, the women cried out: *'Ezzy yellalah!'* For God's sake, sister, enough!

This would go on all night. Towards morning the washer of the dead would come and prepare Zinibe for her burial. She would be bathed, perfumed, painted like a bride, and finally clothed in her finest garments, bright silks that must have emphasized her loveliness.

Mohammed and Kalipha called for me next morning. I was not at all sure that I should attend the funeral. A dread of giving offence filled me with misgivings, even though Kalipha insisted that I would unquestionably offend the family if I stayed away. Outside the mosque, waiting for the service to begin, stood a group of men. Sallah was among them. It was a brilliant morning, but rather cool, and he was wearing his white burnous over his head as bridegrooms do in the marriage procession. 'May Allah bless the household,' we said, pressing his hand. I felt painfully out of place. I would go home. Kalipha would have to explain that I had come only to give Sallah my sympathy. But Kalipha had taken him aside and as they talked both glanced my way. After a moment he called to me and the bereaved husband said very kindly: 'You are a friend of the family, Mademoiselle; it is also commonly known that you are a friend of El-Islam. Go into my house without fear that you are an intruder.'

Zinibe lay in state in the middle of the sun-flooded court. The bold green and red stripes of her winding-sheet mocked the austere draperies of the women who flowed in and out of the rooms, or huddled wailing about the bier. An arm shot out and pulled me down against the wall beside Kadeja. Boolowi, who must have been getting pretty bored sitting there, gave a rapturous crow of delight and climbed into my lap. I had some difficulty making him understand that I could not play. He kept laughing up at me, patting my face to get my attention, and my grave looks and motions, instead of sobering him, excited appreciative chortles, as if this were a new kind of game.

Women kept coming in a steady stream, adding their shrill condolences to the mournful din. The two little boys, Hedi and Bashir, trailed drearily about like lost gnomes in their short white burnouses, the hoods framing their chubby faces. Awisha was everywhere—answering the door, rekindling the fire-pot for the *nahwehe*, holding the baby, passing the water vessel.

Zinibe's face was uncovered from time to time. The jaw was bound up in cotton. It was not a face any more, it was a barbaric mask, for she had been given the traditional make-up of the virgin bride. The brows and lashes looked lacquered, the forehead was finely beaded with black arabesques—the work of painstaking hours—and upon each cheek was a large round patch of vivid pink. So Zinibe had looked on her wedding night when her face was uncovered that her husband might see what manner of woman he had married, so she had looked at the birth of each of her children. And now Zinibe was dead.

'They will lower her into the curving bier,' sobbed the *nahwehe*, 'and singing they will bear her across the plain. Ah-Ah-Ah!' When the women in the court were sufficiently aroused, she moved to the adjoining rooms and stirred up all impartially.

We sat and sat. It seemed to me, at least, that the men would never come. Once again they were uncovering Zinibe's face. The two oldest boys had come in, and now, one after the other, Zinibe's children—Ali, Mohammed, Awisha, Bashir, and Hedi—laid a kiss upon her ornamented brow. The litter was carried in by Sallah and Kalipha. It was a trough-like barrow decorated with copper nail-heads. The women gave way to frenzied grief at sight of it. Shrieking, wailing, they lifted the body and laid it upon an oval mat of woven grass which had been placed beside the couch. In this it was lifted to the barrow. A wooden frame was then fitted across the middle and over this was flung, canopy fashion, a pall of many colours—gold, green, salmon pink and vermilion. It was gathered at the ends with large safety-pins and a broad velvet sash of bright purple was bound about the whole.

When the hearse was ready, Sallah and Kalipha hurriedly spread mats about the court, and the women took themselves into the rooms. Boolowi and I remained in our places against the wall. When the women had closed themselves from sight, the men poured in, exultantly chanting. The various religious orders were all singing different chapters of the Koran, singing to burst their lungs. It was the powerful noise of the marriage procession—tumultuous, discordant, exhilarating. Four of them picked up the litter, the throng surged toward the street, followed by Zinibe in her brilliant palanquin borne high upon the shoulders of her carriers. The doors burst open and the prostrate women staggered after it to the very threshold. They needed no *nahwehe* now to muster their tears. This was sincere sorrow, as if they realized for the first time that Zinibe was gone.

Kalipha, Mohammed, and Farrah were waiting for me at the door. We had to hurry, for the procession was well in advance of us; on account of Kalipha's club-foot we never quite caught up with it. Through the narrow streets it wove, triumphantly singing. Under the busy gate, and out upon the vast sun-warmed plain. Jemma Towfeek, the little mosque toward which we were heading, reposed placidly among its scattered tombs. The bobbing cherry-red fezes, the snowy burnouses, the lusty voices bawling Allah's praise, and, like an afterthought, in the rear, the tossing palanquin, its colours so splendid in the sunshine! Its carriers were constantly changing, for anyone who wishes to expiate his sins may help to bear the bier. At short distances, consequently, there was a scramble for its handles. Up the road, then diagonally across the plain to Jemma Towfeek we swept.

Kalipha thought best that I should wait at the mosque during the interment, so Mohammed and I seated ourselves on a bench outside the door. The loud ringing voices gradually receded—the grave must have been at least half a mile away—until they were just a faraway, sweet tone upon the silence. Several times I had chanced to be wandering in the cemeteries at the time of a burial. I knew just how the shrouded body would be lowered deep down into the narrow brick chamber prepared for it, how logs would be laid across the top to support the roof of bricks and cement, how earth would be shovelled over it and packed and levelled.

The events of the morning had brought vividly to Mohammed's mind the death of his grandmother, Meneh, who lived on like a hardy perennial in the hearts of her family. But the little boy spoke of her playfulness, her drollery, how some evenings she would keep the family circle doubled with laughter. His own rang out fearlessly at the recollection. I thought I had never heard a better sound! For pure delight I joined him. It was wonderful to be laughing together like this! Something hard and tight and very dry inside me was relaxing, expanding. I begged him to tell me more about Meneh.

Before very long we were aware of voices down on the road. In scattered groups the men were leaving the cemetery. Presently Farrah and Kalipha came up, and we reached the road in time to be among the last stragglers. One of them was Zinibe's Mohammed in his rust-coloured burnous, hiking home all by himself.

The men were ready for a smoke, so we stopped at the first café we came to. We sat quietly drinking our coffees, facing the cemetery where Zinibe lay waiting for the two fearsome angels, Munkar and Nekeer, who would descend, any moment now, to examine her concerning her Faith. 'Ah yes, my friends,' sighed Kalipha, abstractedly. And then, as if to himself, he added, 'Today it is Zinibe, and tomorrow—which of us?'

THE MONTH OF
ABSTINENCE

S idi Ramadan is coming to those who smoke and pinch snuff! a little
girl sang teasingly as she skipped down the street. The patrons of the
coffee-house smiled at one another. The Month of Abstinence was hardest
on them. To do without food and water from daybreak until sunset was
one thing, but to do without coffee and cigarettes was almost more than a
man could bear. Ramadan! The Holy City talked of nothing else! Days of
piqued faces and short tempers, of lassitude and street brawls, but the
nights, ah, the halcyon nights of feasting and conviviality! Glorious
Ramadan—ninth month of the Moslem calendar—when the Prophet
received the first revelation!

Kalipha was the happiest man alive when I mentioned that I was
thinking of keeping the fast. My reasons did not interest him. 'Yes, yes, I
know, that is what you say!' Smiling wisely he tapped his brow. 'This
thing has a thousand explanations—very practical, very wise. As a writer
you want the experience, then, because your money has not yet arrived,
you are obliged to economize. All this is very well. But Allah, who knows
the heart, is not deceived. Ah, *ma petite*, how often have I said that you are
a Moslem? Here is proof! If you were born into the Faith you could do no
more' He laughed joyously. 'Abdallah, Eltifa—how the whole family will
rejoice! The women will raise the *zaghareet—Alla-la-een! Alla-la-een!*—
like that. And the city! If Kairouan honoured you before, how much more
will she honour you when it becomes known that you are *Sima
Ramadan!'*

This lively prophecy rather staggered me. In vain did I argue that
my observance would in no wise be religious. Kalipha could not, would
not understand. It was futile to pledge him to silence or even to the exact
truth. The most solemn vows and adjurations would not hold him from

broadcasting his 'triumph' and reaping the sweet fruits of public approbation. An alarmed silence fell between us when I declared I would give up the idea. After a time Kalipha said, very seriously: 'But this is not necessary! Observe Ramadan for whatever reasons you wish; it will be recorded in any case. And if I am asked why you keep the fast I will say, "It is Mademoiselle's way of showing her respect for me and my religion."This, surely, is no lie?' It was, at any rate, far enough from downright falsehood, as well as strict truth, to enable us to compromise.

The day before the beginning of Ramadan is called *Leylet er-Rooyeh*, The Night of the Observation. Bedouins thronged the streets, the plain between the city walls and the cemeteries was speckled with their tents, which seemed to have sprung up overnight like mushrooms. The coffee-houses—even the meanest cubby distinguished with the name—prospered. The fryshops, those appetizing pockets in the walls, were freshly whitewashed, their copper kettles scoured to the ultimate brightness. During the afternoon, about the time that they close their shutters for the day, the friers were busy making honey-coils and other Ramadan fritters. Gaily painted candy carts we had never seen before were trundled through the streets. The minarets all over the city were hung with tiers of little black cruses that waited only for the dusk to bloom. But quite apart from the visible signs, there was something in the air—something piquant, and tantalizing, soberly festive. *'Sidi Ramadan est en route!'* said Kalipha, who every day during the past week had given us a whimsical account of the good saint's preparations, his visit to the baths, the packing of his suitcase, and so on. In fancy, I saw a little man, pulled sideways by the weight of a large yellow suitcase, hiking furiously across the plain.

Towards sundown watchers appeared on the balconies of the minarets, the roofs of the baths, all along the city wall scanning the west for the new moon that would proclaim the beginning of Ramadan. Kalipha, Beatrice, and I joined those who were watching from the sand hill outside the city. The sun had set, the *muezzins* had called the prayer, a strong wind was blowing and the men, their chins buried in their burnouses, sat hunched in quiet groups. A few shafts of orange were all that remained of colour, the hills below were fast deepening to violet. Above the sombre cloud banks a blue star, the bedouins' star, Kalipha always called it, glittered, a very prince among the twinkling pin-points.

But where was the bright little crescent? The first to spy the herald would run at top speed to the Kadi and the boom of the cannon would officially pronounce it Ramadan. The populace would converge at the Mosque of Sidi Okbah for the service, whose solemnity and importance were surpassed only by that commemorating the birth of the Prophet.

We left the knoll absorbed in its vigil and hurried to the mosque, for Beatrice and I would not be allowed there later on. The vast columned nave was as bright as a ball-room. Great lanterns hung from every arch and the celebrated candalabra, composed of multitudes of glass cups with floating wicks, were glistening pyramids down the central colonnade. On stockinged feet we padded among the smooth and fluted pillars—glorious shafts ransacked from all the empires of antiquity to uphold this great Islamic shrine. Although it was early, worshippers were scattered here and there, fathers sat with their sons, a few small boys were having a merry game of hide-and-seek, old men moved their lips in prayer, a mother swathed in black led in her little ones, off in an arcade a knot of women conversed quietly through their veils.

We were on our way home when the cannon sounded. Like an echo a muffled roar sprang up from the city and lingered for many minutes. Kalipha, who had come to a halt, shouted: 'Bless ye the Prophet! On Him be the peace!' We hastened to the main street, where all was noisy and bright and gay as Broadway at the stroke of midnight on New Year's Eve. Everybody was shouting, 'O blessing! Blessing! Bless ye the Prophet! On Him be the peace!' 'O followers of the Best of Creation—fasting! Fasting!' 'Fasting tomorrow, ye sons of Islam!'

What a change from the Kairouan we had known all the winter! By nine o'clock, ordinarily, the population had retired within doors and every reminder of vivid, impetuous day had given way to stately silence. The *souks* were locked, shop fronts dark, street stalls empty. The main street was deserted save perhaps for a little flock of women shuffling home from the baths or a lone man making for the warmth of some favourite rendezvous. Coffee-houses were snug dens of sociability and in the stygian blackness of by-streets occasional chinks of light hinted of women at their looms, of tea and story telling.

But Ramadan turned winter to summer, night into day! Business hob-nobbed with pleasure in the brilliant corridors of the *souks*; in coffee-houses bordering the market-place bedouins sang to their flutes; the main street gleamed with shop lights, flowed with promenaders wearing musk or jasmine over their ears. In sequestered lanes and quarters the women, too, were celebrating—the thump of their little pottery drums, their shrill merriment defying locked shutters and bolted doors. While high on the minarets those tiny flames, which the wind had spared, fluttered valiantly. Long after Beatrice and I went to bed the singing, the clapping, the plaint of mandolines from the coffee-house below mingled with the happy voices of the promenaders.

I have no idea at what hour the revelry subsided, but when, quite suddenly, I found myself awake, Kairouan was deep in sleep. In a dream Munkar and Nekeer had visited me accompanied by a corps of grisly djinns beating drums and blowing upon little goat-skin bagpipes. Even now, and I was positive that I was awake, I could hear the hollow *boom-boom* of the diabolical skirling. Afar off, but coming nearer, slowly, taking their time, steadily, with fateful certainty. I lay very taut, though reason scoffed at my fear. Supernatural rubbish! About as supernatural as your straw mattress! The strolling drummers are abroad rousing the city for its last meal. Kalipha warned that you would hear them before daybreak. 'Awaken! Awaken!' the tom-toms and *zukarrahs* are saying. 'Partake of *sahoor*! Eat and drink until ye can discern a white thread from a black!' Now they had turned into Kalipha's lane and were advancing toward the street. Passed the Bath of the Bey, passed *Numéro vingt*, where Mohammed, Kalipha, and Fatma lay under the same blanket, passed the public oven—I cowered under the bed-clothes as the lurid racket climbed through the bars of my window, filled the room, and, before I actually died of fright, moved gleefully off down the street.

I awoke next morning vaguely disturbed as by the memory of a nightmare. Even before I opened my eyes I sensed that Kairouan was changed. By half-past six the noises of traffic, commerce, and industry are welded into one terrific roar, the component parts of which are lost in the monstrous orchestration of street sounds. But all was strangely quiet this morning. *Dang-dang-dang* every stroke of the copper-smiths hung upon the bland air. '*Caka! Caka breema!*' a solitary bread-boy piped his little *roulade*. Camels groaned and farther down the street a jackass, the legendary cause of their grievance, started honking, while a confused chanting informed me that there was a Koranical school in the neighbourhood.

No good listening for the slap of Hamuda's slippers on the stairs—Kairouan had settled down to Ramadan. With the dreary realization that there was to be no coffee this morning, nor tomorrow morning, nor any morning for an entire month, I crawled out of bed. For the life of me I could not understand why I had gone in for Ramadan; my stomach growled its resentment, the more so when I heard Mohammed delivering Beatrice her breakfast. *'Bonjour, ma soeur!'* he knocked at my door and all radiant came in to wish me good of the fast. He himself was observing it for the first time in his life. Weeks ago he had announced to the family that he was no longer a child; this year he was going to keep Ramadan. As he was under no obligation to do so for two more years at least, they neither discouraged nor encouraged him. Abdallah's face, however, betrayed his delight, Eltifa, motherly soul, could hardly approve, but she would not have dreamed of interposing in a matter that was, as Kalipha observed, entirely between Mohammed and Allah.

This morning, in his own eyes at least, Mohammed was a man. That uneaten breakfast had for him all the significance of a boy's first shave, his first long trousers. Satisfaction glowed deep in his merry eyes, and crept out of the corners of his large mouth when I intimated that I recognized his new status.

'Ah yes,' he sighed, 'in a few more years—three at the most—you will find me bringing up the marriage procession.' I asked if he had decided upon Halima, the daughter of his patron, but Mohammed was no longer so sure that his old playmate was his choice. Lately a friend of his father, a wagoner from Sousse, had been teasing Mohammed about one of his daughters. Half in jest, half seriously, he told of her charms, her accomplishments, always referring to her as 'your fiancée.' Mohammed went him one better and spoke of 'my wife,' and although these conversations were more or less in the spirit of fun, he was plainly coming to think of her as practically his. Like a chicken that is destined for the table of the bey, his Fatma was in her little cage over there in Sousse being nurtured and fattened especially for him, Mohammed ben Kalipha.

'Three chests will not hold the linen she is bringing me!' he cried. 'Yesterday her father gave me this good advice, "Listen," he said, "work hard, save your sous, and before you know it, my friend, I will be driving you to Sousse to sign the marriage contract!"'

'But you do not know this girl,' I said, forgetting for the moment that the idea of love as a basis for marriage is incomprehensible to the Arab mind, 'and you do know Halima. Wouldn't it be safer to marry someone you have always liked?'

'Halima is very nice,' Mohammed admitted. He swung his bare feet in silence for a few moments. Then his face brightened. *'Ma femme* can read and write in French as well as Arabic! She can also embroider, as well, I believe, as any woman in Sousse. Sidi Amar swears that it is impossible to find words to tell me of her beauty!'

'Halima is beautiful too,' I insisted, 'and although she has never been to school, she can weave and cook.'

'I know,' he said sadly, 'it is very difficult.' There was time to decide, I observed. Then, by way of reminding him that he had been a long time from his work, I asked if he had begun to save. The question rushed him to a subject much nearer his heart—the three-day fête that brought Ramadan to a close. Oh, the fête-the fête-the fête! The clothes he would wear! He had bought himself a *shakakah*, a little pottery bank, and every night he would deposit two francs, his wages for the day. Yellow pantaloons he would buy himself, and a complete set of embroidered vests (he drew his hands over his thrust-out chest), then a robe—of silk perhaps—new slippers, a tasselled fez—*'une coutûme complète, ma soeur!'* he laughed joyously, *'même un mouchoir dans ma poche pour fantasie!'* It was the thought of such finery, as yet unearned, that sent him scuttling back to the market-place.

Everything was off schedule today, or rather, on a new one. Kalipha, who always made a point of being on hand to supervise the cleaning of our rooms, slept away the morning, in consequence of which it was nearly noon before I heard the swish and knock of Ali's mop. On the other hand Beatrice, whom I almost never saw until supper-time, dropped in. She had a fist full of brushes, the inevitable blur of paint across her cropped hair. She had been standing behind her easel, she said, a cigarette in her mouth, when Ali shambled in. He had made the bed and had started on the floor when he uttered a loud cry, down clattered the mop, and the huge fellow rushed out of the room, his hands to his face. When he came back he had a towel bound about his nose and mouth and with signs and shrugs and apologetic laughter he explained it was the cigarette smoke, one intentional whiff of which would erase all the merit of the month's grim fast.

I had no mind for my work today. The little irregularities and interruptions tempted me to truancy and the terrace outside my window had an irresistible pull. Now and then a street brawl—an inevitable accompaniment of the fast—slowed up the traffic as everybody stood vacuously about until the stormy altercation was settled. An occasional donkey weighed to the earth with household furnishings elicited shouts of praise from passers-by. Of all months Ramadan is deemed most propitious for marriages and the common sight of a bride's dowry on the way to her future home never fails to evoke cries of 'Bless ye the Prophet!' Several of the shops set deep in the shade of the pepper trees across the street were closed. The bread-counters and the date-stalls along the curb displayed their wares as usual for, Ramadan or no Ramadan, invalids and children have to eat. There were less city folk, more bedouins in the throng, particularly bedouin women, their draperies, strong lapis to begin with, faded to every exquisite shade of blue, their head-dresses flaming orange, hot red. There was colour, noise, movement enough in that vortex, Lord knows, and yet to the practised eye it was not quite the customary hurly-burly. A certain amount of work had to be done and so people moved about and did things, but they all felt as I did—languid and a little light-headed.

During the afternoon Kalipha showed up and we sauntered through the town. Cafés and fryshops were closed. The bey's fortune could not buy one a cup of coffee or a fried cake. In the hushed *souks* work went on in a desultory fashion or did not go on at all, for many of the shops were shut until nightfall. We killed an hour or so calling on Kalipha's friends—Sidi Shedlie in the perfume *souk*, Sidi Amar a leather worker, Sidi Salah Najar, a scion of one of the old aristocratic families, but a simple tailor, for all that. They had heard—leave it to Kalipha—that I was keeping the fast. '*Sima Ramadan*?' they asked me bashfully, as if to confirm a report too good to be true. 'I swear by Allah,' was Kalipha's prompt and proud reply, '*Sima Ramadan!*'

This sort of thing bothered me dreadfully at first. My insistence upon an explanation mystified Kalipha. 'But they do not demand your reasons!' he protested. And it was the truth. My motives interested them no more than they had Kalipha. It was a fact, wasn't it, that I was *Sima Ramadan*? Enough. Praise be the Prophet! Such warmth and faith gradually cleared my conscience of hypocrisy. This experience which I was sharing with them was bringing us humanly closer. They were my friends, they trusted me. I had gained more than a set of lively impressions and sensations, something infinitely precious, more enduring. Perhaps, I reasoned, there was, after all, something 'religious' in my observance.

The City's pulse was very low by three o'clock in the afternoon. We walked across the plain to the Mosque of Sidi Abdelli, where Kalipha's parents were buried, and sat on the little blue-tiled pavement above Meneh. While Kalipha talked of her and of his father, the strenuous Kassem, the red sun was going down, down toward the horizon. 'But come!' he cried abruptly, glancing at the sun, then at his watch. 'We must be quick if we are back before they call the prayer.'

Kairouan, in the meantime, had shaken off its torpor. Everything was alive and exciting, waiting for the signal from the minarets that the day's penance was done. Coffee-houses were ready for business, the fry-shops were piling up mountains of honey-coils and crisp breakfast cakes, little girls darted home from the public ovens with covered bowls on their heads, the beggars under the Great Gate had never been so importunate, vendors wearing trays of cakes or carrying pitchers of coloured syrups praised the Prophet and their merchandise in the same breath. We found seats outside Hamuda's stall. The tables were set with jugs of water, and now, as the moment approached, every man had an unlit cigarette between his fingers. The sun had set. The *muezzin* was already on the balcony of the little mosque next door. Every minaret had its solemn figure watching the turret of the Great Mosque for the flinging out of the red flag. '*Allah Akbar!*' A burst of song came down to us, the rest was blurred by the joyous bellow that leapt from the crowd. Cigarettes were lit; water and coffee could come after. The tension slowly relaxed, serenity and good humour were restored. Our first meal, the *fatoor*, which Kalipha had prepared before leaving the house, awaited us, but we were in no hurry. We sipped our coffees leisurely as the blue dusk thickened and the bats swooped over the street.

Kalipha had decided that Beatrice and I were to have our dinners at his house during Ramadan. His master hand exceeded itself on those feasts! And then the delightful evenings around the fire-pot or in the coffee-houses, a number of which had special Ramadan attractions. Professional storytellers held forth in some, continuing from night to night the same wondrous stories. Bedouin music drifted from others, in Ali's large touristy café near the entrance to the *souks* the bagpipes of the snake charmer squealed. Below our hotel, in the back rooms of the restaurant, some imported dancing girls cut mighty swathes in the profits of the courtesans who occupied the little dead-end street against the city wall.

Because of me, the family did not wait until just before daybreak to eat the last meal. After midnight Mohammed would fetch from the oven across the street a pair of roasted sheeps' heads or some other delicacy which Kalipha had prepared as a surprise. Abdallah, whose tea was especially in demand during Ramadan, and Eltifa, who had engagements for almost every night in the week, were both home by this time. Abdallah was not too tired to brew another pot of tea and to tell us one of his rather austere little stories of warrior saints and miracles, nor was Eltifa too dead-beat to regale us with the innocent gossip which she had accumulated during the evening. This was the best time of all, I used to feel!

The last half of the fast is generally considered to be the hardest. There is no longer any novelty to street fights, the combatants can be killing each other but the heedless crowd moves on. I, like everybody else, was wearing 'the face of Ramadan,' and for the first time in my life I had no hips! Perfect strangers came up to me with the question, by now so familiar, 'Is it true that you are keeping Ramadan?' to which Kalipha with proud dignity would reply: 'You will find the answer in her face.'

As the fête approached a motley flock of harbingers appeared—toy merchants, flower, candy, and sherbet vendors, bizarre clowns and magicians. Old Bab Ali, the travelling tumbler from far Morocco, was welcomed back to the marketplace.

But Kairouan's chief thought was clothes. The coffee-houses buzzed with talk of new turbans, vests, *gondorrahs*. Every day we must visit the *souk* of the tailors to see how Kalipha's street-robe—blue with black stripes—was progressing. The *souks* at night were very brisk. Fathers brought their children to be outfitted. When the costuming was completed, the *shakakahs* were broken on the customers' seat, the contents counted, the money proudly paid—the benign fathers making up the difference—and, after coffee or pink syrup had consummated the transaction, the little peacocks marched home carrying their neatly folded purchases like love-offerings.

Ah, yes, good *Sidi Ramadan* was preparing to depart. He was patching his shoes, mending his garments, brushing his fez. His visit had been a happy one, it had seemed so short, he would be missed, but oh the joys of the fête! The marketplace would wear the panoply of carnival—swigs, whirligigs, and whatnot. For a sou a child could soar like a bird, or ride madly off to Zanzibar on a wooden horse! The streets would sing with new raiment and promenaders would kiss shoulders in festal salute. The women would visit the cemeteries, there to spend the daylight hours without molestation or supervision. Striped tents would be erected over the graves of those who had died during the past year, bright rugs would enliven others. It was not only a reunion with the dear dead, but a convivial old-home-week compressed into three short days. There would be a tent over Zinibe's grave, of course, and from dawn until dusk her loved ones would sit beside her, and, when at last it was time to go home, they would set a lighted candle in the little niche of the head-stone to keep her company through the night.

Before sunset on the last day of Ramadan an old man with a brown chaplet in his hand wandered through the town exhorting the Faithful to watch for the new moon. But they were already on the roofs, behind the crenellations of the City wall, on every promontory that gave them a limitless view of the sky. Perhaps I imagined that there was a special glory in the setting of the sun tonight, perhaps it was only the consciousness that millions in Egypt, in Morocco, in India, Arabia, and Persia were watching with us. As if regretfully, the sun sank at last behind the hills, and in a few minutes the Call filled the air with sweet sad music, but, although it meant the end of the long fast, it rose, swelled and died this evening without huzzahs as the children of Islam gazed silently, steadfastly toward the glowing west.

INTERLUDE

There had been a serene timelessness about the winter—no Sundays to make us conscious of the passage of the weeks, no Christmas, New Years, or Easter, no need at all for clocks and calendars. Time had been meted out to us in one fair piece. Beatrice's departure—for it was understood from the first that she would leave for Brittany in the spring—was always in the future. Things would go on like this forever, it seemed, and as if afraid of prematurely destroying this illusion, we avoided the subject of parting. *'Ne me dites pas de ça!'* Kalipha would implore when it came up. 'It is not necessary to set a trap for sadness; it will come of its own accord too soon.'

It came, consequently, with incredible suddenness. Kalipha and I accompanied our friend as far as Enfidaville, the first stage of her journey. There was a constrained moment of handshaking, another of boisterous blessings and reminders, and we were left watching the train rush self-importantly across the plateau and rapidly diminish, until it was just a mote upon the horizon. When even that had whisked away, we turned and walked back to the station.

There was nothing in sight to justify the low white building—no village, no human habitation, nothing but plain and sky, sky and plain; the horizon encircled the drowsy little Gare d'Enfidaville like an immense hoop. Kalipha had brought our lunch along—a casserole of liver and chestnuts and a chunk of Eltifa's bread. He was as happy as a child on an outing. Not that he wasn't sorry that Beatrice had left—he defied anyone to say he wasn't sorry—but the train ride, the picnic, the prospect of a long afternoon in the soft spring air and the journey back to Kairouan in the early evening were not to be wasted on futile regret. Singing, jigging his shoulders, he spread a napkin on the ground, uncovered the casserole and divided the bread. He ate with more than his usual gusto. 'How beautiful the air is!' he cried, pulling in great draughts of it. 'What silence! Not a sound, not a movement. It is as if we were alone in the world!'

Never in my life had I felt more so. I made a dismal pretence of eating, but the food would not go down my throat. In the end, without a word of remonstrance, Kalipha ate my share as well as his own, and, except for a surreptitious glance from under his shaggy brows, he gave no sign of noticing my abstraction as he endeavoured to divert me. Finally, when we were having coffee in the *buvette*, he ventured plaintively. 'You are very calm, *ma petite*.' The whole afternoon lay ahead and he did like his friends to be gay. 'No need to tell me why,' he commiserated, taking my hand, 'for I am sad, too. You should have seen me this morning in the midst of the packing. The tears came, I could not stop them. I cried,' he raised his hand in a so-help-me attitude, 'I *cried!* And Mlle Beatrice, she comforted me. "I am the one that should cry!" she said, and I swear, my little one, there were tears in her eyes!' I had to smile at the picture of that sudden burst of sorrow, of Beatrice's consternation, her timid awkward attempts to console him. 'But what do you wish?' he went on with a profound sigh. 'Life is like that. When the moment comes—one goes, for who can escape his destiny?,' And he was launched upon one of his interminable, somewhat vague discourses, only half heard, in which he compared terrestrial separations to the Last Great Departure, allowing a *little* chagrin to be fitting and natural. Grief was like a tap. You could switch it on or off, or you could turn it so that there was a moderate flow, neither too much nor too little—just enough to keep the heart moist but not the eyes. For what-was-to-be-gained and was-it-not-wrong . . . Did I understand? 'Yes, I understand.' I replied absently. 'But it is easy to talk.' I saw instantly that I had said a terrible thing. His face froze into an oblique smile of bitterness. 'You mean to say,' he said, 'that I mind our friend's leaving less than you do?' It took a good many more coffees to straighten *that* out! But when it was finally settled that his loss and my loss were absolutely equal, we found a sunny sheltered bank out on the plain, Kalipha made a pillow of his burnous and promptly went to sleep, and I opened Beatrice's parting gift, her own copy of the *Odyssey*.

There was nothing casual about our homecoming that evening. The family had apparently been given instructions to do their utmost to cheer me, for I was given a heavy welcome. Mohammed came running with his arms up, Fatma rained kisses, Abdallah sent in with his compliments a round of mint tea. Eltifa, who was leaving for a *fokkarah*, came to the threshold in her black *haïk*, clapping her hands and chirping: 'Welcome, O Rose! Welcome, little sister!' Then, thinking to make me laugh, she croaked in what was meant to be Beatrice's contralto: 'Eltifa, the jasmine! Eltifa is a gazelle of El-Yemen!'

But after dinner we all 'had djinns.' Mohammed, rebuked, flung himself down and went to sleep, Abdallah, for reasons known only to himself, kept strictly to his own household, Kalipha caught Fatma making faces at him and in a black rage grabbed up the first thing he could lay his hands upon and clouted her around the court. My intervention brought his wrath down upon me. '"Make a little Patience" you say,' he stormed, throwing the punitive instrument, one of his wife's wooden clogs, into the corner. 'What have I been doing for the last two years? For two years— nay more than that—I have put up with her shiftlessness, her stupidity! I have explained, I have coaxed, I showed her. All softly I encouraged her, telling myself: "She is still young, she will learn." But it was not for nothing that the husband before me divorced her! Good God, how I am afflicted! *"Faite un peu de patience!"*' He smote his forehead. 'I have used up all the cloth! Of what shall I make this "patience"? Tell me.' Then, clasping his hands, he glared at the ceiling and in a loud voice implored Allah to change his luck.

During the ensuing gloom, he smoked one cigarette after another, darkly turning over in his mind how he could rid himself of his 'affliction,' while I, on my side of the fire-pot, was thinking of the evenings with Beatrice. The best of them had been spent in this little room. What peace, what serenity there had been, fuller and sweeter for being shared with such a friend. A friend with whom one could be comfortably silent for hours, who when we conversed caught the most delicate shades of one's meaning. It had been good to look up from one's book upon that tranquil semicircle, Eltifa with her distaff against her knee, Fatma beside her picking over the raw wool or carding the washed fleece, Abdallah, in his accustomed place behind the fire-pot, listening with quiet amusement to Mohammed's animated chatter; on one side of me Kalipha smoking his kif-pipe, Beatrice, on the other absorbed in *The French Revolution*. 'Listen to this,' she would say. At such moments of intense admiration there was more gold than brown in her eyes. From Carlyle's heroic prose we would drift, ruminatively, to talk of other things. I was going to miss the stimulation of those evenings. No book, no matter what I was reading, was as interesting to me as Beatrice's conversation. She was utterly devoid of sentimentality and sham, her words stood for something, just as every stroke of her brush was thoughtful and honest. She was younger than I; it was true she knew the world better, but that large enlightenment of her mind, which distinguished her from any other person I had ever met, had nothing to do with age and experience.

Kalipha threw his cigarette into the fire. *'Allons!'* he said brusquely, getting into his burnous. *'Au café! Il faut chasser ces djinns qui nous embettent!'*

The day after Beatrice's departure, at Kalipha's suggestion, I took her room for the summer. The whitewashers came with buckets and ladders, and by afternoon, the walls were dry enough for me to move in. But it was not the simple shift that Ali and Kalipha supposed it would be, not a mere matter of carrying in my table and suitcases. For I had suddenly found that I could no longer be tolerant of bed-bugs.

All winter, fired by Beatrice's hardy indifference, I had scorned to let them worry me. If she could rise above them, so could I. We had been brought up, of course, in the belief that they are shameful vermin, necessarily associated with filth, and yet, the Arabs, who were not a dirty people, had bed-bugs and thought nothing of it. After all, I told myself, they were not scorpions or cobras. What could a few little bugs—even quite a lot of little bugs—do to me! By such reasoning, I did actually succeed in ignoring them. (A recollection that will always give me a certain satisfaction.)

But, with Beatrice gone, my borrowed stoicism collapsed. I felt that I would rather die than sleep another night on that loathsome bed. It was a complete victory of matter over mind. First of all, I threw out the mattress. Then, having got Ali to take the iron frame apart, I went to work with a blow torch which Kalipha had borrowed from a smithy. In the meantime, the men, who were not to be trusted for thoroughness, stood by exchanging amused glances. Their complacency switched to horror, however, when, after the bed had been fired and put together again, I began making it up without a mattress. I was not going to sleep like that, was I? Just a folded blanket between me and the springs! *Hullah-hullah-*

hullah! In an agony of dismay, Ali lugged in, one after another, the mattresses from every bed in the hotel. Kalipha implored, beseeched me to let the women make me a new one. But how could I be sure that bugs wouldn't get in during the process? No, I preferred to sleep on the springs. And to tell the truth, that little iron cot, cleansed and purified by fire, had for me, at the moment, all the appeal of the most luxurious bed in creation! But there was no convincing Kalipha who had worked himself into a state of helpless fury. There was such a thing as going *too* far! 'Now what are you doing?' he demanded suspiciously. I was pouring kerosene from my lamp into four little tins. Curious as to what precautionary measure this might be, he watched as I set a can under each leg of the bed. 'Y'Araby!' he groaned when he finally caught on, and clapping his hands to his head, he laughed until I thought he would break a blood vessel.

I liked to move about in my spacious, bare, clean room. It was blissfully cool too. From the hot glare of the street it was like stepping into a cave. Soon the heat would be too intense to stir out of doors much during the day, yet my windows would make it impossible for me to feel myself a prisoner. In the other room, I had been obliged to run to the terrace to see what was going on in the street, now all Kairouan was right beneath my windows. I could look deep into the shops across the way, the little mosque opposite was a starting-point for processions—marriage, circumcision, and funeral—and there, in full view, was the great double gate, the old arch and the new, side by side, auricles through which the life-blood of the ancient city poured tempestuously, unceasingly, in and out.

There was no reason, that I could see, for me to dread the summer. My money had come before Beatrice left, and so little had our living cost all winter that, after paying my debts, there was money enough to carry me well into the autumn. By now the fever which Kairouan had induced in me had subsided and I was back at work, transcribing and submitting to magazines the stories Kalipha had told us. For human intercourse, I had Kalipha's family; every day since Beatrice's departure had carried me inevitably, without my, realizing it, deeper and deeper into their concerns. Moreover, I had Beatrice's letters to look forward to—magnificent, characteristically vigorous letters, each an event to be discussed for days. And before she left Paris for Brittany, she sent off a box of her books. Mindful of how we had husbanded the few we had between us, she sent none of your 'slim' volumes to be tossed off in an evening, but Romaine Rolland, Sévigné, Thackeray, Proust and Fielding. Let the long summer come! Entrenched in clean surroundings, among people I loved and trusted, with money enough, with work to do and books to read—it had no fears for me.

THE LONG SUMMER
(EXERPTS FROM MY JOURNAL)

May 1st

Only eight days before *'el-Eed el-Kebeer,'* The Great Festival! Kalipha pounded upon the door this morning before I was up. I was told to dress quickly, not to wait for coffee: there was buying and selling of lambs for the sacrificial feast. I scrambled into my clothes and we made our way to the *fondook* at the outskirts of the market-place. The massive courtyard was already crowded with victims, but more were being driven in, their lumpy pink tails hanging like shawls from their backs. I have never heard such an uproar—the bleating, the baa-ing, the frenzied bargaining! Mohammed, shining with self-importance, strode up to us with the announcement that Sidi Hassein, his patron, had commissioned him to buy two fat lambs for the fête. He led us through the sea of grey backs to show us his selection. Kalipha plunged his hand through their wool and felt their heavy tails. 'You have not chosen badly,' he said, secretly very pleased. While we stood there the patron himself appeared and approved of the choice. Then Mohammed was radiant!

We had our breakfast under the pepper trees alongside Hassein's shop. Mohammed sat upon the round mat he was making. His needle, a curved strip of polished wood, threaded with braided strands of dried grass-sped in and out. No need for his master's *'Feesa! Feesa!'* Faster! Faster! Today Mohammed was, at least, the junior partner.

The fête was already in the air. Men discussed their purchases, and how much of the carcass they would give to the poor. The Koran prescribes three-fourths, but in this decadent age, according to Kalipha, it is customary to distribute 'several morsels' and keep the rest for one's family.

May 9th

The first day of the Great Fete! All morning the street has been a rainbow of children bound for the market-place. The girls in their long *futahs*, the brilliantly striped shawls that bind their hips, look like little women. Most of them are barefoot, some wear coloured slippers, some clogs and silver anklets. Others teeter along in ludicrously big French shoes. A few have compromised and are wearing clanking anklets *plus* the high-heeled shoes.

Small boys go in for the gimcracks that make the most noise—trumpets, snappers, firecrackers, ratchets, drums, bells, and whistles. The happy tumult of the market-place fills the whole town, but grown-ups are indulgent. 'Let them, let them!' laughs Kalipha who ordinarily hates a rhythmless racket, *'el-Eed el-kebeer* is principally for the children!'

The streets last night were tense until the cannon boomed. Then the mandolines, the singing, the syncopated clapping began. The fête was on! Coffee-houses had been given permission to remain open all night. They brimmed with gaiety—their own peculiar brand that is never obtrusive or rowdy. The main street had become a cheerful lamp-lit passage across which the clients of rival coffee-houses conversed. The lanes and by-streets, a spooky catacomb through which one hurries after dark, were starred with festive doorways.

We visited all our favourite cafés, drinking innumerable coffees, teas and syrups. Convivial lights rimmed the market-place, one whole side of which was being converted into a playground. They were setting up the rickety paraphernalia —the swings, the little Ferris wheel, the valiant wooden horses. Children who should have been in bed ran about gleefully anticipating the dawn.

In the dim crypt between the double gate, which is a saddle *souk* by day, bedouins were gathered and one of them was singing to the flute. They have their own songs, even their own mode of singing. There is an eerie, haunting quality to their voices—a quavering far-off sweetness—as if they were singing under the water. To the same weird little melody the boy improvised endless stanzas, borrowing his themes from his delighted auditors. He sang the praises of one man's new burnous, of another's horse that had excelled in the last Fantasia. As we took seats in the ring he wove us in, welcoming 'Madame' and 'Courage,' not neglecting to mention the nosegay over his ear.

All at once the music stopped. The town criers were abroad; all ears were cocked for the pronouncement. It was decreed that the women should visit the cemeteries during the morning, the men in the afternoon. Any man found there out of hours would be imprisoned. The order was received with unanimous approval, and the boy took up his song.

Kalipha was all for making a night of it, and he probably did after I went to bed. I slept but little, however, for the carnival beneath my window never flagged and at daybreak I awoke to the same joyous hubbub, only now it was the children!

May 17th

It is the time of the pilgrimage. The Holy City is full of strange faces, men who have journeyed here from all over northern Africa.* They are conspicuous for their new-looking raiment. 'Voilà a pilgrim from Gabes,' Kalipha will remark, 'notice the way he is wearing the burnous? And there are three from Touggourt!'

'But how can you tell '

'Sometimes by the burnous, sometimes the robe, but mostly by the headgear. Voilà, le turban de Sousse! C'est chic, n'est-ce pas ?'

During the week or two that they remain, they are lodged in the precincts of the Mosque of Sidi Sahabi, in the courtyard of which a coffee-house has been set up for their diversion. Favourite taverns are neglected these evenings; the men all flock to Sidi Sahabi.

Late one afternoon, days before the influx, we were sitting outside a coffee-house at the outskirts of the City, idly watching two figures approach by the road that crosses the plain. They were carrying staffs, coming slowly as if they were footsore. 'Pilgrims from Morocco' exclaimed Kalipha as they limped toward us. 'Praise the Prophet!' They stopped at our table and asked for directions and water. They were barefoot, darkened by the sun, their white garments grimed with dust—they had been two months and a half on the road! The spokesman was skinny, short, rather negroid; his talk sounded strange to my ears. Even Kalipha had difficulty understanding the dialect. The taller one, of finer features, kept his eyes on the City as Kalipha pointed their way and instructed them to ask near the Gate for their fellow-

---

* The Great Mosque of Kairouan is deemed one of the four great sanctuaries of Islam. It is a favourite goal of pilgrims from Barbary

countryman Abdallah, the Tea-maker. We gave them our good wishes and watched them trudge across the market-place and pass beneath the ancient gate that had admitted so many thousands like them.

While Believers pour in by bus, train, caravan and automobile, there are only a few from Kairouan this year on pilgrimage to Mecca. The long drought early in the spring has impoverished the City, so that, instead of the usual exodus, to her shame and sorrow, there is only a handful. With envy we hear that a small place of prosperous olive trees is sending five hundred! One of Kalipha's cousins, an elderly man who has put by all his life for the sacred journey, left this morning amidst a mighty fanfare. Months ago he arranged his worldly affairs as if he did not expect to return. He drew up his will and appointed Kalipha the guardian of his family during his absence.

We were invited to his home last night, the eve of his departure. Mohammed and Kalipha joined the menfolk at the mosque and Eltifa, Fatma and I went directly to Sidi Ali's dwelling where scores of women were gathered. The usual curiosity, I was passed around, handled, and screamed at—on the supposition that if they shout I will surely understand. Eltifa found an opportunity to whisper that Kalipha's first wife, Aisha, was present. I spotted her at once, a large, rather florid woman who kept rolling her eyes at me as if to say, 'Oh, the things I could tell you!' With each new set of arrivals there was a flurry, a jangle of welcoming cries, and I escaped to a corner where two little boys made room for me. They were dressed alike in crimson robes. We were admiring one another's clothes, they the fur on my collar, and I, the crescent-shaped pockets on their miniature vests, when there was a rush for the stairs, the women scrambling into their *haïks* as they fled. The men were coming! I was hauled up and away to the roof where we knelt around the low parapet looking down upon the court. I was surrounded by phantoms—black and white shapes crouched or standing in startling groups against the starlight. 'If only Beatrice were here!' I kept thinking.

It was a tremendous farewell! The large court filled rapidly. There was all the turbulence of a marriage procession, the shouting, the shrilling of pipes, the throbbing of tom-toms. Turbans and fezzes formed a ring eight or nine heads deep. One well-wisher after another stepped briskly into the centre to chant a single line, whereupon the rest would heave a mighty chorus, while the aerial cries of the women fluttered off in ribbons.

My knees were raw by the time the men finished with a lusty prayer that all the guests assembled might experience the bliss of pilgrimage to the tomb of the Prophet.

This morning the pilgrims were conducted to the station; thousands of them from all over Tunisia will embark tonight on the same boat. Kalipha says that everybody is talking of something that happened as the procession swept through the town. One, Sidi Gadoona, a draper, sitting before his shop, dashed in and got his money, locked the door, and even as he ran he was putting on his street-robe to join the future *hahj* on their fateful journey.

June 4th

Yesterday I learned with dismay that Baba Hahj has been hurt because I have not yet visited his household. So it was arranged that this afternoon I should make my call upon his wives.

Papa Hahj, or 'Babelhahj,' as we call him, is probably Kalipha's closest friend. He is a likeable little man with a quick smile and merry eyes. There is nothing about him, however, except of course his title, to indicate that he has performed the sacred pilgrimage, or, that he is, as Kalipha insists, 'very, very religious.' The other *hahj* I have met dress only in white and with the honoured prefix have assumed a certain sobriety and dignity, neither of which distinguish Babelhahj in the least. His size and his humorous face are against him. Then, too, he is such a little dandy! His big gaudy turban makes him look top-heavy, his street robe is always conspicuous for its stripes and now that mustard-coloured, mail-ordered shoes are the fashion he is sporting a pair.

Babelhahj occupies a unique position in the eyes of the menfolk of Kairouan for he has achieved the impossible: conjugal felicity with two wives under the same roof! 'How does he do it?' I have often heard them ask. Kalipha has told me as much as he knows of his friend's affairs. Babelhahj has been married to his first wife, Haleema, for over twenty years. Their one child, a girl, died at the age of twelve, and Haleema never succeeded in bearing another. In her compassion for her husband she implored him to take another wife, but his respect for her was such that for years he refused to do so. She was overjoyed when he finally consented to marry Macboobah, a much younger woman, who promptly presented him with a daughter and is again pregnant. All summer I have hoped that Babelhahj would invite me to visit his remarkable household, only to learn that he is offended because I have not done so!

He and Kalipha escorted me to the house. (The latter, of course, did not enter, but waited for us in the café across the road.) In the entrance passage a little girl came running to fling herself into Babelhahj's arms. Obviously, she had been dressed up for this occasion. An uncouth Western frock-all open work and ribbons-hung below the tops of her buttoned boots; on her head was a rakish pearlstrung fete cap. The women were in the court to greet me with outstretched hands and a cordial 'Welcome in the name of Allah!'

Babelhahj explained that each wife has her own complete household. I was first taken into Macboobah's, a spacious room, as clean as wax. The doorway, the windows, the bed, were hung with spotless curtains; Kairouan carpets brightened the tiled floor. As in every Arab home that presumes to be at all *de luxe* there stood the ugly French dresser and upon it the inevitable flowers under a glass bell, but it was nice to find the whitewashed walls adorned with warrior-saints on smoking chargers.

I felt extremely self-conscious sitting above them on the only chair; I missed my little interpreter and almost regretted that I had refused to let Mohammed beg time off from his work. In desperation, at last, I abandoned my high seat and joined them upon the floor. I think we all felt better. Their French is even less than my Arabic, but we talked—now that I think of it, it's amazing the ground we covered! I learned that Kadusha is two years old, that she adores her crystal hat and never willingly removes it, that her mother wants her to learn to read and write. I was told, too, that Haleema's brother is a letter-carrier; that the women had woven the rugs upon which we sat. They demonstrated how one sits in front of the loom weaving, while the other embroiders in back. I, in turn, told them—don't ask me how—that I am single and alone, that I write stories for children, and that I love Kairouan. We got on famously! Then we crossed the court to Haleema's house. The low table, which they now set before me, was covered with a towel. 'How Mohammed will mourn!' I thought, as Macboobah lifted the cloth disclosing dishes of home-made cakes—mealy *baklowa* with flaky crusts, date-stuffed *mahkroods*, and little cones of short-bread. My 'Share in the name of Allah' provoked only urges to begin. One is always expected to eat in solitary state, *'kief-kief sultana,'* (like a sultana) as I expressed it, which made them laugh and pat their chests with pleasure. Haleema brought the tiny cup and saucer, where upon Macboobah must jump up to fetch her rosewater with which to flavour my coffee. That set Haleema rummaging for her scent and I was drenched with amber. As I ate, there was an easy, pleasant flow of conversation among my host and his wives; Kadusha sat between her two mothers watching me. I suspect that Haleema is a bit indulgent for when I offered Wistful-Eyes a cake Macboobah smiled and shook her head, but Haleema, with an Oh-come-Mother-just-one look, let the little girl choose which.

Parting was blissfully easy. No hysterical pledges of life-long devotion, that generally make Arab leave-takings so tedious; these women simply took my hand and asked me to come again.

Babelhahj and I joined our friend in the café. Impressed with the quiet harmony in that home, I asked Kalipha if he thought I knew Babelhahj well enough to ask him his secret. Kalipha, amused, put the question without cogitation. Babelhahj seemed not at all displeased. 'Well you see it's like this,' was his whimsical reply, 'I tell Haleema in confidence, "An old love is like an old fez—it's comfortable." And to Macboobah I say, "The love of a maiden is like jasmine over the ear." Then each wife, believing that she is the favourite, can afford to be generous to the other!'

June 12th

We have formed the habit lately of strolling out beyond the ramparts to the *fondook* just before sunset. It is good to get away from the racket. We sit on the stone ledge outside the little coffee-house and the profound stillness of sky and plain gather us in.

Tonight, Babelhahj and Sallah, a mutual friend, who were promenading along the road that skirts the city wall, strolled across to join us. Atop their slopes, strewn white with tombs, the Mosque of Sidi Arfah and Sidi Abdelli were hallowed silhouettes against the sun. The moon, like a pale petal, lay upon the sky, there was a ruddy light on the backs of the camels, a peach-bloom upon the ramparts. The women were already leaving the cemeteries; I could see their veiled figures, some black, some white, picking their way among the little domes.

While Kalipha and his friends talked together I amused myself watching the bread-man I see so often around the *fondook*. He is a short, amazingly sturdy, broad-bottomed fellow in prodigious green bloomers. His red moon face is humorous, and there is scarcely a tooth to his smile. The gaudy bandanna around his head is knotted in front and the ends, sticking up like horns, give him a decidedly jaunty air. Sallah, catching sight of him started to laugh; something he said made Kalipha and Babelhahj chuckle. *'Sidi Makmood! Ya Sidi Makmood!'* shouted Kalipha, then turning to me he explained, 'Attend! You are about to hear an amusing story. This Makmood is very droll!'

He stalked over to us—he walks like a prize-fighter—and cheerfully seated himself on the edge of a chair. He needed no coaxing to begin, but if he made his story brief, he apologized, it was because the sun was nearly gone. (Bread-stalls are busiest right after the sunset Call to Prayer.) In less than five minutes he left the men roaring. This was his tale.

He was the youngest of fourteen and he worked with his brothers in the fields. At noon one day he came back hungrier than usual. *'Ya Ummi!'* he called to his mother, 'Is there something to eat ?'

'In the *kassar*,' she responded.

He uncovered the great bowl and found *erfeesah*, a pudding made of oily cake crumbled in the mortar, then mixed with dates and sugar. He ate and he ate until he had eaten half the *erfeesah*. He was still hungry, but he clapped the cover upon the rest.

'Well, my son, have you eaten?'

' *Elhamdullah*.' Praise be to Allah.

'Have you eaten enough?'

'Well—I could have eaten more.'

'Then go back, my little one, and satisfy your appetite.'

So back he went and finished the pudding, after which he stretched himself in a corner of the court and went to sleep. Presently his eldest brother returned. He, too, was ravenous, and Ummi referred him to the *kassar*. He lifted the lid. 'Do you mock me!' he shouted, 'the *kassar's* clean as if the cats had licked it!'

This is strange cried his mother, who came running. 'Only the little one has eaten.'

So Makmood was aroused and forced to confess his knavery. He was contrite, but his brother was merciless. 'You *eat* for fourteen; have you the *force* of as many?'

'Yes!' retorted Makmood for the taunt roused his dander. He remembered that there were twenty bags of grain outside, and that three hands had been detailed to load them after lunch. 'Come, I will show you!' Makmood marched into the yard, his brother following him.

Twenty hard stout sacks, their ears up, reposed in ranks against the wall. It would have taken two men to lift and pitch each bag. Makmood picked up the first, held it for a moment above his head, then hurled it into the cart. Lift-pause-heave, he had disposed of another. His brother stood watching him, nor made he any comment as sack after sack fell into position. When the last was loaded Makmood brushed his hands: 'Now you see why I eat for fourteen?' His brother bent and saluted him with a kiss upon his forehead. Then taking a five-franc note he folded Makmood's fingers about it, saying with a smile: 'Take the rest of the day off, and finish your dinner!'

June 24th

Kalipha and I have our favourites among the *muezzins*, but I have a special fondness for the one that calls the prayer from the little mosque across the street. From daybreak until dark he regulates my day, and during the night, in that dead hour before there is a footfall, before the chink of Hamuda's coffee-tins, even before the metallic *tank-tank* issues from the fry-shop on the corner, the sonorous voice of my *muezzin* awakens me. For twenty minutes or more he extols the perfection of Allah—leisurely, with long pauses, as if he had a great joy up there in the black sky with the white city spread in sleep below him. In the absolute stillness that disembodied voice—rich and resonant—reassures me like the cry of a night-watchman, and I go back to sleep, though I always mean to hear it to the end.

Late this evening we found ourselves in the vicinity of the Grand Mosque when it neared the time of the *Adan*. This quarter is assuredly one of the blackest, the single street-lamp as feeble as a glow-worm. We crossed the common and stood leaning against the wall, our eyes near the summit of the minaret. For some reason or other we spoke in whispers. Any moment a light would flash the signal to hundreds of *muezzins* in readiness on their dim towers. We hoped that the boy would be the one to give the Call. Above all the other voices, perfunctory, tired, sorrowful, vigorous, or serene, his shrill soprano soars, imperious as a challenge.

A couple passed within two feet of us, the white bundle walking, not before or behind, but with the man; decorum can relax on the by-streets. 'What was she saying?' I whispered as they stepped under the light, and were presently swallowed by one of the lanes. She must have been returning from the baths, for Kalipha caught the remark : 'I'll change to the other, where one is sure of hot water.'

I kept imagining that I saw a shape on the balcony. 'It might be,' murmured Kalipha, 'he waits ten minutes for his signal from below. Ah see!' It was the light. Then *'Allah akbar!'* (Allah is great), breathed Kalipha. Another moment, the Call itself—not in the boyish shout, but the plaintive, sweet tones of an old man. Turrets, far and near, took up the exhortation, the heaven was filled with jagged music. The light continued to flicker, though the others be calling, each *muezzin* must see the signal. Near and far, turret by turret then, the sounds died to gossamer echoes as the *muezzins* turned to descend. The spark, above, went out.

Kalipha explained as we walked away that whatever you may be saying when the Call goes up must be received as gospel. "Ah, you see," a man can say, "I speak the *truth*!" So many a dispute is settled by the intervention of the *muezzins*.

THE LONG SUMMER
(CONTINUED)

The Arabs are totally destitute of feeling for animals. It is significant that they make no pets. A dog is a guard, no more; a cat catches mice and scorpions; pigeons are to keep the court clean of crumbs, while the donkey, his slender legs splayed under burdens that would break the back of a horse, his sides covered with scabs and sores, fiendishly branded with barbaric arabesques, expects and receives nothing but savagery. The other evening at the *fondook* two lank cows were driven past us at a gallop. I turned away, positively sick. 'What's the trouble,' Kalipha asked blandly, my sensibilities being a source of endless wonder to him. 'Is it because they are flogging those cows? But that doesn't matter, *ma petite*, they are on their way to the slaughterhouse.'

The day before yesterday the black cat had her kittens. There were four, but two were born dead, and the third 'fell down the well.' Last evening when Mohammed brought up my supper I asked about the last one. 'He's dead,' said Mohammed, setting the things on the table.

'Oh how?'

Mohammed shrugged his shoulders. He had accidentally stepped on it.

'Mohammed!'

'Yes, it's a pity. But he was very little and the court was very dark.' Another shrug. 'Oh well!'

Later Kalipha and Mohammed called for me and we walked along their street on our way to the Place Finou, a cool little common where we often spend the evening. Past their house, on a refuse heap at the side of the road, a minute cat was crying piteously. It was crawling over the filth, with staring weak blue eyes. Father and son quickened their steps; I stopped.

'But this is *your* cat—the one that died!'

'Oh, leave it, leave it. It will die presently.'

For a few moments I walked on confused, then I began to be furious. They had never heard me talk so, but they took it in silence. Even to my own ears my voice, in the narrow street walled with stone dwellings, sounded enormous. At last Kalipha stopped and threw out his hands, 'But what would you have me do!'

'Go back, you wicked man, and put it out of its misery!'

They both flinched. Mohammed kept very still.

'That I cannot do,' Kalipha confessed shamefacedly. We walked on. We had seated ourselves on the Place, our coffees were brought, and I was still going it. I think Kalipha was afraid I was going to make a scene, for he suggested, very gently, that I go back with Mohammed. So, setting down our cups, we returned the dark length of their street. As we approached the refuse, the little boy's steps lagged. There wasn't a sound. Hope flew into our hearts. At first I couldn't find it. But there it lay, no bigger than a mouse. I stooped to make sure it was dead, and it stirred. Mohammed fled shrieking up the street. The needle-piercing cries started up again. Passers-by began to gather, a tall boy was about to oblige me by stamping upon it, but I pushed him against the wall. (I can still see his look of amazement from the shadows.) Mohammed had come back, very tentatively. I put the cat in my handkerchief and sent Mohammed ahead to fill a basin with water.

Drowning a kitten sounds trifling, but may I never have to do it again! Fatma and Mohammed lurked about, ghost-ridden, as I prepared the washbasin. I wouldn't have believed it possible that a kitten, even now half dead, could make such a noise! My hands were shaking, but I locked my teeth and plunged him in. There wasn't enough water and his head kept struggling out of my grasp to emit a terrified shriek. Mohammed in the corner covered his ears and groaned. Fatma, tittering like a zany, handed me water from a distance. It was awful—that frantic struggle under my hand. I had to hold him down finally with a cloth. Bubbles kept coming to the surface. Bubbles, more bubbles. Finally they stopped. 'Is he dead?' whispered Mohammed. A prolonged silence, then again, 'Is he dead?' After a few minutes more, we filed downstairs and emptied the basin upon the rubbish pile.

Kalipha's glance, as we came up, was a curious mixture of

amusement, wonder, and respect. After a while, after he had made sure that I was again of sound mind, he ventured with a sly twinkle, 'This night you have shown us that there is another side to your tongue.'

'Yes,' Mohammed chortled, exuberant at the recollection, 'and it is like a razor!'

July 20th

Two months are gone and the *hahj* are returning. Welcoming crowds meet the trains with banners borrowed from the mosques, great glass lanterns borne upon heads and shoulders, tomtoms, tambours and pipes. We are told that we cannot expect Hahj Ali for another fortnight. Upon disembarkation, he joined a small party of zealots that proceeded to the *Kaabeh* on foot—a perilous journey over desert and mountain. They reached the Tomb eleven days after the others.

Kalipha came this morning to tell me that one of our *hahj* died on the voyage home. Kalipha knew him well, an elderly man who lived outside Kairouan in the gardens of Drat Tomar. The boat paused at a port only long enough for his son to take the body ashore and leave instructions for its burial. The womenfolk, who had received no word of his death, were among those at the station today. 'Oh, how terrible for them!' I cried.

Kalipha shook his head, 'No, my little one, it is not "terrible"; it was this good man's destiny. For a time the women will wail and scratch their faces, and we will pardon the weakness. But it is inestimable bliss to die while performing the pilgrimage. Would that it could be the lot of every Moslem!'

August 12th

Last night I had an awful scare. It was late—almost midnight—and I sat working at my table. The street was alive with promenaders enjoying the air, deliciously cool for a few hours before dawn. I could hear Kalipha's voice; he and his friends were occupying one of the benches against the ancient gate. I sat chewing the end of my pencil when, out of the tail of my eye, I saw something flick across the wall. I held up the light. There it was, motionless, a little curve of ivory with head upraised and jewel eyes. I almost dropped the lamp. 'Kalipha! Kalipha!' I shouted from the window. 'There's a scorpion in my room!' I dashed out to summon Ali. When I got back the thing had disappeared. Then I saw it on the window-frame. I tried to get it down with the broom-stick and it whisked behind the wash-stand. As I prodded about I heard a tiny sound, an infinitesimal twitter, and it lipped across the floor, paused an instant beneath the bed, and vanished. Ali and Kalipha burst in with anxious faces. They set to work searching every crack and crevice. They shook the garments hanging on the door, they pulled the bed apart. Ali found it finally in a chink of the floor-tiles near the door. He held it up by the tail—it swinging frantically, eyes a-glitter—and the men had a good laugh. 'That's not a *scorpion*,' cried Kalipha, 'that's a harmless little lizard!' Ali shambled out with it to the terrace. 'Tomorrow' Kalipha promised, 'I will get you a cat. Then you need have no fear of scorpions.'

Sure enough, I have a cat—a leggy kitten, as black as a djinn. Kalipha objects to my calling him 'Djinny': that would be inviting trouble. So until I decide on a name, it's "Kitty" or "Pussy." Kalipha refers to him as "Kiddypussy," so this may come to be his name.

Because I might forget, I must record this on the subject of scorpions: A few nights ago we were sitting outside the coffee-house at the far end of the market-place where we can look out upon the starlit plain. "Look' said Kalipha, startling me out of my reverie. He pointed to a low light creeping toward us from the direction of the market-place. *'Sidi Mohammed fait le bien!'* Now up, now down, nearer and nearer, the light searched the wall as it came. In its wake was an old man, with an antique lantern in one hand, in the other a giant pair of pincers. Behind him strolled a half-grown coloured boy with a long pin upon which had been transfixed at least a dozen scorpions. Tagging this ghoulish pair were the inevitable hangers-on.

This old gentleman, it seems, this searcher of walls by night, gave up a lucrative business in the *souks* some years ago to pursue scorpions. Along the ramparts, in the courtyards, through the coffee-houses, all evening every evening during the summer, he travels so throughout the town.

'But who pays him?' I asked incredulously.

'Nobody. He does it simply for *le bien*.'

'But if he is, as you say, a poor man?'

'Oh, this one gives him two sous, that one a franc, someone else fifty centimes, and many give him nothing.'

'And that is how he lives?'

'Yes, he has only himself. As he says, "A morsel of bread, a cup of coffee, and *hamdullah!*"' Kalipha kissed his hand and reverently touched his brow.

The little band had gone on, but they would pass our table on the way back. I was instructed to have a coin ready. Kalipha hailed them and they paused in the dazzle of their great lantern. Sidi Mohammed's restless eyes kept wandering over the wall in back of us as the coloured boy solemnly laid the pin across our table. It squirmed with a thousand crab claws and legs. Those scorpions were stunning, their jointed tails fashioned from exquisite jots of ivory.

The old hunter itched to be off, so I put my franc in trust with Sambo, and they moved on.

But this is not the only case of devotion to the public weal, *le bien*. Kalipha could cite many instances. He asked me whether I had noticed beneath my window a certain man who sits at the side of the road dispensing water from cans about him. All summer I have seen and heard that man.

He has a melodious but interminable chant, 'Quench thy thirst in the name of the Almighty!' I have never seen him pocket a coin; he just sits there in his battered fez calling and handing up his little pots. Every other person accepts one, drinks, hands it back, and passes on. I had decided that it must be holy water from the Mosque of Sidi Okbah, an explanation that didn't altogether satisfy me.

'He does that for *le bien*—that's all,' Kalipha assured me. 'He has no parents, no wife, no children. One gives or does not give; it is all the same to him. He gains his loaf, his cigarettes, and a corner in the *fondook*—it is all that he requires. But Allah, He knows! It is certain that this man will be admitted into Paradise.'

August 8th

Hahj Ali is home again! His son met the boat at Tunis, and on Thursday a telegram informed Kalipha that they would arrive in Kairouan on the *Jemma*, or Sabbath. Characteristically, Kalipha was all for a tremendous demonstration at the station. With the telegram in his hand, he rushed out to inform the family and round up a crowd. He was terribly crestfallen to find that the Hahj's closest friends, without exception, advised against an ostentatious welcome. Kalipha was also very much disgusted. 'No tom-toms, no pipes, no songs! *Mon dieu*, it will be like a *Roumi* funeral!' He had half a mind to go ahead with his plans, but Abdallah finally succeeded in persuading him that such a display would be discomfiting to the serious Hahj Ali. So decorum was reluctantly decided upon. A selected group would meet the train at noon and quietly conduct Hahj Ali to his mosque.

On the morning of the *Jemma*, Jannat, her small grand-daughter Bayia, Mohammed, in his best tasselled fez, and I went to the home where the women were preparing the traditional dish, the *asséedah*.

There was no mistaking the house. Red ochre and whitewash proclaimed it to be the dwelling of a *hahj*.

The court was a spangle of colours; vivid headkerchiefs, velvet bodices, holding high and partially exposing the breasts, long white pantaloons, and striped hip-scarves. Children, like so many imps, darted about getting slapped and screeched at by their *ummis* who were making infinitely more noise as their fingers flashed against their teeth in *zaghareet*, the melodious but piercing joy-cries.

We were taken first into the dark kitchen-cubby, dense with acrid wood-smoke. On an improvised hearth of stones sat a cauldron filled to the brim with white mush. It was heaving and sucking ponderously. A woman was stirring it, her purple *takritah* was damp with sweat, for it took all her strength to force the pole through the pudding. From time to time she wet the top of it so that a crust should not form, and when it lopped over the rim as it boiled she whisked it back with her hand. The women were taking turns at the stirring for the blessing it insured.

Jannat mingled with her friends in the court. Mohammed went tearing around with the other hoodlums and Bayia, who kept a firm hold on my dress, watched them with solemn eyes. Evidently, this was not Bayia's idea of a good time, so we strolled into one of the rooms and sat ourselves down in a flock of little girls. They resembled a collection of heathen dolls, their hands and feet stained the yellow-red of henna; their foreheads, arms and fingers elaborately stencilled in black. They were chattering like the sparrows in the pepper trees at sundown. It was not long before Bayia and the child next to her were comparing their ornamented hands. I've no doubt that Bayia was very envious, because while most of them were miniature editions of their mothers, her friend had on a European dress—a hideous pink thing—and instead of the kerchief, her braided hair was stuck about with small blue bows that simply wouldn't stay on.

The room was packed with women, the bed—a high, canopied shelf—accommodated at least ten of them. They were chewing loban, a resinous gum, or snipping the toasted seeds of pumpkin. And babies! I counted sixteen, but I'm sure there were more. Drab mites, all apparently born at the same moment, all remarkably alike, and remarkably ugly!

From where we sat I had a grand view of the court, the vortex of the activity. The pavement was rapidly being sown with pumpkin seeds, there were shrieks of laughter as a woman rode another's shoulders. Somebody was always thumping upon a pottery drum, and a few were always attempting the stomach-dance, whereupon the *zaghareet* would soar above the noisy laughter. At the rhythmical *dum-dum-dum* of the *darbooka* the babies jumped in their mothers' arms and a two-year-old in purple got to her feet and began to sway in perfect time, clapping her paddies above her head.

A little bedouin girl seemed to be the leader of the children. A black-figured *takritah* bound her short dark curls. She had a piquant face with a wide, humorous mouth and gleaming teeth. Her skin was the old gold of her tunic and as she romped, her drapery, held together at the shoulders with safety-pins, flew apart at the side revealing her lithe little amber body. There was the instinctive beauty of the dancer in all her movements. Breathless with running, at last, she sauntered into the room, caught sight of the sedate city girls, and pounced upon them. 'Ya Ka-*dee*-dja!' they protested, laughing in spite of themselves, pushing her away lest she spoil their finery. 'Ya Ka-*dee*-dja!' she mimicked them, dodging their blows. She baited the Pink Girl particularly until there were screeches for '*Ummi! Ya Ummi!*' Laughing, Kadeja pirouetted a few times. Suddenly she dived, plucked out all the blue bows and showered them upon the outraged young lady! Then there was a tussle from which Kadeja emerged with ecstatic giggles and the Pink Girl with tears and unbecoming language.

Dum-*dum*-dum, dum-*dum*-dum! At the beat of the drum the madcap whirled into the court and started to dance. The women stopped to watch her. Her bare feet scarcely moved, she swayed like a golden flower, her left arm arched above her head, her right hand cupping her ear. A young bedouin woman, who was watching her with amusement, pride and delight, tossed her a bright handkerchief. They were so much alike that I assumed her to be Kadeja's sister; instead she is her mother. How she stood out among the city women! In her indigo drapery she might have stepped from an Etruscan vase. Her child has her body, the same freedom and elegance of step and gesture. Her red and yellow *takritah* was knotted carelessly over satiny crisp black braids, her silver car-hoops were strung with crude piebald beads. I think I shall never forget that intelligent quizzical face. It was good to hear her robust laughter!

Most of the afternoon she held herself aloof from the merry-making. Once I saw her unashamedly asleep in the passage-way, once, standing against the wall, relaxed, one knee bent, her blue drapery revealing a sculptured thigh. When she felt like it she danced, and when she danced the court was hers. Not even Kadeja could compete with Mabreeka! She was obviously a great favourite, but to me she seemed an alien, a roving Ceres among the blatant city women with their loose figures, grotesque make-up, and trumpery raiment.

The trilling of the *zaghareet* now, announced that the *asséedah* was done. Massive bowls of it were being set upon the court and there was a mad rush for places. On the top of each snowy mound was a deep well of oil; to one side was a pile of powdered sugar. I quickly caught on to the trick of eating it. First you scoop up some with the first three fingers of your right hand, then you dip the hot lump into the oil, next into the sugar. It was delicious—like hominy in consistency, with a rich flavour as of crushed nuts. Over in a corner the blind musicians, who had been engaged for the afternoon festivities, had a *kassar* all to themselves.

When they had finished, a fire-pot was brought and, after they had heated their drums and tomtoms, they got down to business. With seraphic bliss the women sat about as the minstrels shrieked the songs sacred to the return of the *hahj*. At frequent intervals everybody joined in a deafening chorus, '*Hahja, hahja inshallah! Hahja, hahja inshallah!*' If it be the will of Allah, may each of us become a *hahja*! Just how, above this din, it was learned that Hahj Ali was at the door, I will never know. There was a prismatic whirlwind around the entrance-passage and the poor man, his turban askew, was strangled and wept over by forty or fifty hysterical women, while the musicians banged away at their drums! He stayed but a moment, for which I could not blame him; the men were to enjoy their *asséedah* in the mosque.

The furore had not abated when a donkey bearing a sack of gifts from 'the Holy territory' was ushered into the court. Mohammed and his friends were honoured with the unloading. Nobody dreamed of prying into that mysterious sack, but it was the subject of excited conjecture for the rest of the afternoon. Kalipha has since told me all its contents— comerry, a perfumed wood for incense, frankincense or liban, prayer-beads of aloes-wood, pellets of dust from the Prophet's tomb, phials of water from the sacred well of Zem Zem and, for the women, black powder or *kohl* for the eyes, and *swek*, a fibrous wood that, when chewed, colours the gums and lips. Kalipha, after quite a struggle with his conscience, finally gave up and told me a secret: Hahj Ali wants to make me a gift of a little of the incense. As it was to have been a surprise, I am cautioned to simulate astonishment, even to ' cry with joy' if I can. I don't believe I shall be able to do that, but I can act as I feel, sincerely touched and pleased.

August 13th

The relative calm of mid-afternoon had settled over the torpid street. I sat at my table trying to keep my mind off the rivers of perspiration that were coursing down my body, when a smothering sensation took hold of me. For one frightened moment I thought I had been overcome by the heat. I went to the window. Blasts of hot air were pouring in. The desert wind, the *scericou*! I thought, only this wasn't a wind, it was like the emanations of some mighty invisible furnace. The street was deathly still, waiting, transfixed, for the thing that was about to happen. An unearthly light, a dense musk yellow, hung over the entire city.

The sand-storm came with a terrific rush. It was all I could do to bolt my shutters. Through the mustard smudge I could see the bread merchants scrambling to cover their stalls, a man on the roof of the baths ripping frenzied towels from the lines, muffled figures dashing for shelter, objects flying down the street, the pepper trees writhing. In another moment everything is blotted out, the panes in my shutters are twin plaques of bronze. The heat strangles me, the shutters belly and strain at their lock, the yellow dust from the Sahara piles upon the sills, covers my table, my nose and throat are parched with it. I clap my hands to my face in order to breathe. Thunder-crash after crash—then the rain, a slanting drive of great drops that quickly puts out the dust. Once more I can see through my windows. Domes, minarets, and roofs are still coloured gold by the strange twilight, the pepper trees still rush with the wind, their feathery fronds, pink with berries, streaming like ragged banners. The rain comes down, but the sky in places shows a feeble blue. The street fills again, burnouses hang from the heads, faces shine, *'Haneek elkeer!'* everybody tells everybody else, I felicitate thee upon the riches of the rain! One Arab, stepping high to avoid the puddles, carries a faded green umbrella. He looks somehow very comical. Kalipha comes stumping jubilantly up to discuss the *scericou* and together we watch from my opened window. This saffron light intensifies and sharpens every colour note and detail. The melons glisten, the pepper trees are sun-shot emerald, their grapes a riper rose, the ancient gate stands out as if embossed and I am aware, for the first time it seems, of its hoary beauty and grandeur. The White City is silver, fawn, smoke-grey, mauve, biscuit, cream, ivory, pearl, every shade of white. My eyes are delighted with the strawberry of the bobbing fezzes, the quick green of a head-shawl rippling in the wind, a purple vest, the chrome yellow of many pantaloons. The air, moist and vibrant, cleanses our lungs. 'Ah, my little one,' sighs Kalipha, 'Allah is very good.' The rain has been hardly enough to fill the furrows among the paving cobbles, but the street has an amazingly swept look.

The beggars are hunched in their accustomed places awaiting the call of the *muezzins*, the vendors have tuned up; small girls, now that the rain has stopped, clatter by, bearing upon their heads covered vessels or bread from the public ovens; three boys dash down the street dragging behind them a fallen branch as big as a plough. The youth with the watermelon under his arm fits a wedge of it to his mouth.

Across the street on the bench outside Sallah's coffee-stall we watch the sun set upon the immaculate city.

September 5th

Sheaves of golden dates, fresh from the oasis, are heaped upon the curb-stands, the virulence of the sun is nearly spent. In another two weeks or three I shall be moving back into my snug little room off the terrace.

Our chief concern these days is Kadeja. In the spring Farrah took her and Boolowi back to the plain and throughout the summer we heard of them only when we happened upon bedouins from the *douar*. Recently it has come to Kalipha's ears that his niece is threatened with divorce, and my friend is more upset than I have ever seen him. He does not hear half of what is said to him; he walks, sits, smokes, and drinks his coffee in ponderous silence from which he rouses himself occasionally with pious utterances and sighs.

It will not be the first time that Farrah has divorced Kadeja. Twice before he has done so, and twice he has taken her back. But 'not every time the jar is struck doth it remain unbroken,' for if he divorces her again, the wife he loves, and there is no doubt in Kalipha's mind that Farrah loves Kadeja, is lost to him. The Law, as set forth in the Koran, clearly states that a man may divorce his wife twice, but, if he divorce her *a third time* he cannot take her back unless she should marry another and be by *him* divorced. When I suggest that Farrah must know his danger, Kalipha shakes his head: 'The bedouins are like children when it comes to these things. They are Believers, yes, but they do not know nor trouble themselves too much about the Law. However,' he says with a show of resolution, 'we must not despair. To Allah all things are possible.' Yet, whenever he returns to the house he asks 'Kadeja is not here?'

THE STORY OF
KADEJA

Like every girl of decent family, Kadeja, daughter of Sallah, had been reared in the strictest seclusion. She had seldom set foot outside the threshold except to attend the baths or visit the cemeteries; it was a matter of course that no man outside her immediate family had seen her as a maiden. When she was thirteen years old a satisfactory match was made for her. The groom, although a friend of her father, was a stranger to her. She knew only that his name was Bombourt ben Hassan, that he was a coppersmith and the sheik of his guild. Further knowledge must await her bridal night.

Sidi Bombourt proved on this occasion to be somewhat stricken in years, pockmarked and practically blind, but such was her lot—divinely ordained and predestined, to be accepted without question. Kadeja made him a thrifty, obedient wife. The traditional industry of the women of Kairouan is weaving, and a woman's 'value' is commonly estimated to be the sum that the sale of her rugs puts into her good man's pocket; because of Kadeja's skill at the loom she was, also, a profitable investment.

Sidi Bombourt, on his part, seems to have been an irreproachable husband. He had had three other wives, each of whom he divorced on the grounds of sterility, but as the years went by and Kadeja, also, failed to reproduce his image, Bombourt did not reproach her by taking another.

Kadeja was still a young women when Sidi Bombourt died. Her parents were dead, too, by this time and her only brother, Mohammed, had married and settled in Salambo where he had raised himself to the position of steward on the estate of the Bey. Mohammed immediately besought his sister to make her home with him. He had ample means, a spacious villa among gardens that faced the sea; unless she chose she need never remarry.

Kadeja's good fortune was the talk of the hareems. A lifetime of ease and security! Was ever a woman so blessed! Her friends flocked to congratulate her, but Kadeja announced that she had declined her brother's proposal. She wasn't ready for paradise, she said. If she were to enjoy it on earth, how was she to endure it throughout eternity! She would remain with her Uncle Kalipha until he could secure her another husband.

Now widows and *divorcées* are not easy to dispose of in the Moslem marriage market. It must be said in Kalipha's favour that he did not oppose Kadeja's decision, although he deplored the pride that had stood in the way of her welfare. He persisted among the coffee-houses until he found among his acquaintances one who professed to be looking for just such a woman. Beauty, dowry, virginity were not objects of Farrah ben Mustapha's search. He had just divorced his wife and was temporarily through with women, but he needed a housekeeper and a mother to his infant son. If Kadeja bint Sallah was quiet and sensible, she would do.

Sidi Farrah was a bedouin of the Souassi tribe. For generations his family had tenanted Elmetboostah, a *douar* of mud huts several miles out upon the plain. He was tall, even for a bedouin, powerfully built and his lean face was as brown as an antique coin against the snowy folds of his headdress. Kalipha knew him and his brothers to be plainsmen of the finest type, yet he would not have considered such a suit had Kadeja been less anxious to marry. A city girl, in his opinion, was scarcely fitted to endure the hardy, primitive life of the *douar*. But Kadeja made nonsense of her uncle's scruples, so the purchase price was agreed upon, Farrah and Kadeja were married, and the next day, on donkey-back, they set out for Elmetboostah.

It was not often that gossip fed upon such a meal! In the hareems, at the baths, in the cemeteries, wherever women congregate, they gorged themselves on Kadeja bint Sallah's 'misfortune.' Where was her pride now? Gone off on a donkey to live in a hovel! Where was her woman's modesty? She could give her *haïk* to the moths now for the bedouin women have no shame among men. Their faces are naked, their blue draperies seemingly designed to flaunt their slim bronzed bodies. And what a life they lead, *yarsulla!* One relentless round of herding flocks, tanning hides, pitching tents, hauling water, gathering wood; of ploughing, threshing, spinning, milking, and weaving; of travail without assistance of midwife and of exhausting marches in caravan! To be sure, their headdresses, their arms and necks are loaded with ornaments of pure silver, but who would envy them their finery since it is but portable property to be pawned or sold should the crops fail!

If the town women have their opinion of the bedouines, be sure they have their view of the fine ladies of the City. Defiant of hardship, contemptuous of indulgence, the women of Elmetboostah received Farrah's bride with undisguised scepticism. For weeks they watched her for whims and city airs, but Kadeja gave them little cause for censure. She was humble, friendly and not afraid of work, she was a sensible wife and a kind mother to Boolowi. In the emergencies and adversities of the *douar* Kadeja was unfailingly on hand. She delivered a baby with the cool competence of a midwife, she watched with the sick, occasionally she washed the dead. The men liked her for her nimble wit and good sense. They sought her opinion on their affairs and because of her steadfast impartiality in disputes she came, in time, to be regarded as an arbiter.

Farrah, like his father before him, was the village commissary for such small commodities as tea, salt, cigarettes, and spices. But Farrah's easy nature had sadly involved his accounts and he readily turned over the management of the little business to his wife who ran it with an efficiency that was the despair of the casual debtors. When the stock needed replenishing, the intrepid Kadeja would don her *haïk*, mount the family donkey, and ride alone into town. Her city friends were scandalized. 'What do you wish!' she would laughingly protest when they upbraided her. 'Am I the only daughter of Islam whose fate is not engraved on her forehead? For shame!'

Her status as Farrah's wife was exceedingly tentative. It is interesting that Elmetboostah never blamed Kadeja for their domestic difficulties. The *douar* recognized Farrah's weakness, how the most trifling incident at times could provoke him to such nervous anger as knew neither limit nor reason. 'The War put a djinn in Farrah's head,' they said of him, remembering the gentle boy that had left his father's flocks to combat the unknown enemy. Farrah had fought with the bedouin troops throughout the Great War, winning every decoration that the Government of France has to bestow; later he had distinguished himself in the campaign against the Riffs. He had returned home unscathed, apparently, except for the loss of his left eye, but time revealed his scars.

There was no counting the occasions when Farrah, goaded by his djinn, had thrown Kadeja upon the mercy of the *douar*. Twice he divorced her and Kadeja returned to her Uncle.

Kalipha, on principle, always defended the husband. Kadeja must have provoked him—unwittingly, of course. The War had troubled Farrah's head; she must bear with him. When she despaired, let her remember the Prophet's promise. For had not Mohammcd—Allah bless and save him!—given his word that 'When a woman has had more than one husband in this life, she will in the future state, be free to be the wife of him whose character she esteemed the most.' Life is brief; Allah would help her.

The procedure that followed each divorce was always the same. After a decent interval—a week at the most—a delegation from Elmetboostah knocked at Kalipha's door. They were come on Sidi Farrah's behalf to plead for Kadeja's return. Kalipha would put on his dignity to admit them; in stern silence he would listen to their overtures. When he spoke it was to state that he had 'other plans' for his niece. Persuasions, promises, passionate oaths meant nothing to the obdurate Kalipha. For what reason should Kadeja return? To be thrown out again like a painted whore. Really, the gentlemen wasted their time.

But they had come prepared for a long siege. Farrah's guilt was denounced as vehemently as Kadeja's virtues were extolled. This was Farrah's last offence: he had sworn by all that was sacred to Allah. Dawn invariably sifted through the shutters before Kalipha could be prevailed upon 'to relent.'

One afternoon toward the middle of September Kadeja arrived, divorced for the third time. She had little to say as she unwound her *haïk*, but the indignant women were not long in finding the welts and bruises upon her shoulders. They kept at her, plying her with questions until wearily she brushed her hands signifying that she had done. Indeed there was not much to tell. A bottle of cheap French perfume, which Beatrice and I had given her, had precipitated this rupture. The scent had been lilac, cloying, insipid—but it was the mode among the women to disdain such old-fashioned fragrances as amber, musk, bergamot, and jasmine. Kadeja had tucked her treasure among the holiday garments in the painted chest, and so sparing was she of every drop that the perfume might have lasted her lifetime. On the previous morning, however, she had found the bottle empty. Farrah, splendidly apparelled, had ridden off at an early hour with the men of his tribe. That evening, when he returned, the strong odour of guilt was upon him. Tired, hungry, no doubt thoroughly sick of *Haleine des Lilas*, Farrah was in no mood for Kadeja's reproach. Seizing a clog that stood by the door, he fell to beating her and the *douar*, from one end to the other, heard, for the third time, the awful shout, 'I divorce thee! I divorce thee! I divorce thee!'

When Kalipha was shown his niece's bruised back we knew, before he uttered a word, that there could be no compromise this time. He towered above us in the little room like a grim imperator, the tail of his burnous flung over his shoulder, his gimlet eyes flashing fire. 'In the presence of all of you,' he cried hoarsely with uplifted arm, 'I take a solemn oath: May Allah *blind* me, Kadeja, if thou art his wife again!' Farrah's emissaries could pitch their tents in the street below—the trump of doom would sound before Kalipha's door admitted them.

With the greatest stealth and dispatch—for he feared an abduction—Kadeja was bundled off to her brother Mohammed in Salambo.

We never knew how scouts from the *douar* got wind of this *coup*, but Kadeja had not been with her brother a week when Sidi Farrah, himself, appeared at Salambo, chastened, gaunt, arrayed like a bridegroom. With grave courtesy Mohammed made him welcome. Farrah offered no explanation of his singular visit, Sidi Mohammed sought none. The hours, a week, two weeks went by. Kadeja kept to the hareem whose intervening corridors and doors shut out even the sound of her voice. As the weeks lapsed into months, Mohammed permitted Farrah to help him about the estate, but, in all that time, Kadeja's name was never mentioned.

Like most cultivated Arabs, Mohammed was considerate of his wife, the gentle Hanoona, and patient with his children. 'The horse depends upon the rider,' I once heard him tell Kalipha, 'and the woman upon the man. Both are due tenderness and respect.' Mohammed, at any rate, found this policy successful for the serenity of the gardens pervaded his home. I like to imagine those long evenings when, their day's work done, the two men lounged beside the fire-pot. Types more dissimilar could scarcely be found in all Islam. Farrah, product of the plain, illiterate, simple as a child, fearfully proud, and the urbane Mohammed who was privileged to wear the turban of an *ulema*, a doctor of sacred law. What did they talk about, I wonder, as the pipe passed between them?

In the meantime, down in Kairouan, we were basking in the thought of Kadeja's deliverance. Farrah had been in Mohammed's household six weeks before we heard of the situation. The blow almost felled poor Kalipha. His nephew had betrayed him! Useless to remind him that our information had been only hearsay, that we did not know the real facts: Mohammed had betrayed him! He could hardly be restrained from taking the next train to Salambo. Convinced at last, albeit very unwillingly, that his rash impulse would avail nothing, Kalipha washed his hands of 'the whole band' and vehemently spat his disgust.

Kadeja had been divorced early in September. In November, the situation was still the same. By the middle of December Farrah felt himself ready to try again. He rushed to the *souks* and spent recklessly on silks, incense, fruit-paste, festive candles and *several* large bottles of scent. A bus bound for Kairouan was to leave that very afternoon; with Mohammed's consent, Farrah and his dear Kadeja would be in Elmetboostah before nightfall. The plan had Mohammed's benign approval. He did suggest, however, inasmuch as it was Farrah's third marriage, that he should first consult the civil judge for Koranical sanction.

Farrah hailed the suggestion. Spiritually purged, he would not deviate a hair's breadth from the Law! No misgivings assailed him as he hastened toward the Kadi. Divorce and remarriage had always been exceedingly simple. The statement *Entee talikah*, 'I divorce thee,' had rid him of his wife; to get her back he had only to claim her.

Farrah's case was soon stated and he waited uneasily for the Kadi's approbation. But the venerable Hahj seemed to have forgotten his client as he leafed through the worn pages of the 'luminous book.' Presently, fastening a finger on a passage, he cleared his throat and began to recite in a quavering chant, 'Ye may divorce your wives twice: Keep them honourably, or put them away with kindness. . . These are the bounds of God: therefore overstep them not; for whoever over-steppeth the bounds of God, they are evil doers. But if the husband divorce her *a third time*, it is not lawful for him to take her again, until she shall have married another husband; and if he also divorce her, then shall no blame attach to them if they return to each other, thinking that they can keep within the bounds fixed by God. And these are the bounds of God: He maketh them clear to those that hath knowledge.'

Afterward, when we heard the whole story from Mohammed himself, it needed a harder heart than Kalipha's not to be touched by Farrah's torment. With every obstacle that baulked his efforts to find an honourable evasion, Kadeja became more desirable. Dull despair had laid hold of him, however, before Mohammed told him, very doubtfully, that he would see what he could do. He would confer with the authorities. When hope fails, he said, Allah remains, compassionate and mighty.

Mohammed's erudition in Islam distinguished him among the most learned circles of the nearby capital. No one honoured him more humbly than Farrah, but he could not know the force of Mohammed's prestige, nor could he know that a brief consultation with the interpreters of the Law would suffice for the solution of his predicament.

An anxious silence settled over the household upon Mohammed's departure. The women had no inclination to sing at their tasks. Mohammed's sons, as they came and went, cast sympathetic glances toward the still figure sitting against the wall. Except when he raised the carafe to his lips or lit a cigarette, Farrah might have been his effigy in stone. At intervals that must have seemed interminable, the Call to Prayer was flung out across the quiet roofs of Salambo. Food was brought and taken away untasted; from time to time the water vessel was refilled. The lamps were brought at last. The evening wore away until from the dark turrets, the choir swelled the mighty curfew, *Allah Akbar!*

The *muezzins* call only twice during the long night. 'Prayer is better than sleep!' sang the *muezzins* and Farrah knew that it was past midnight. The voices fell and gradually faded until there was only the sound of the sea. The plain goes on living during the dark; a thousand voices, so familiar as to seem one with the stillness, reassures the sleepless bedouin. But the sound of the sea to him is the voice of hopeless desolation. The fire burned itself to ash; one after another, the lamps flickered out. Wrapped in his burnous, Farrah waited for the light. But the longest night has an end; the black sky shivered at last as the *muezzins* heralded the day. Yet the morning did not bring Mohammed, nor did the afternoon. The sun set once more, as reluctantly as it had risen.

The women were at their silent supper preparations when the master returned and found Farrah alone in the lamplight. The exchange of greeting betrayed no concern or excitement; he entered and was received as if he had absented himself for a few moments to attend a neighbouring mosque. Hanoona appeared, bringing his pipe. She took his cloak and Mohammed seated himself, speaking of indifferent matters, while Farrah with steady fingers filled and lighted the pipe and passed it to him.

Mohammed puffed meditatively for a while. 'There is no strength or power,' he said, 'but in Allah.'

Farrah studied the fire-pot before him. 'Ay,' he murmured, 'there is no deity but Allah.'

For a few minutes there was silence. Mohammed took the pipe from his mouth. 'The Prophet—upon whom be the glory—hath said, "Thou needst not raise thy voice for He knoweth the secret whisper and the yet more hidden."' After a pause, he added, 'Nor doth His might exceed His mercy.' Another pause, then, 'Know, my brother, that I have this day consulted the council of the *ulema*.'

Farrah stirred, but he did not raise his eyes.

'It is their decision that the Law is fulfilled if thy wife, for a single night, share the couch of another male.'

Farrah glanced up. Mohammed carefully emptied the pipe and blew down the stem once or twice. 'I have considered,' he reflected as slowly he began to refill the bowl. 'There is, of course, Ali.' He smiled as he mentioned his infant son. 'I do not doubt that he would sleep as soundly with his Aunt Kadeja as he does with his mother.'

A sudden light flooded Farrah's face. 'In the name of Allah,' he cried, 'the merciful, the compassionate!'

That night, accordingly, Kadeja lay alongside little Ali, Mohammed's last-born son. And the next morning, with their brother's blessing, Farrah and Kadeja set out, once more, for Elmetboostah.

HARLOTS

I t was Ramadan again. The little oil lights diamonded the minarets, romancers held their bearded audiences in the palms of their hands. *Shakakas* had begun to jangle, and Mohammed was sedulously saving for a pair of mail-order shoes *'couleur de moutard, très chic.'*

It seemed very natural to me—and to everybody else—that I should again keep the fast. There was no seeking me out with dazzled faces to verify the good tidings; this year it was: 'Mademoiselle is, of course, *Sima Ramadan*? Ay, that is good. There is no God but Allah and Mohammed is His prophet! Thou wilt be recompensed, Brother Kalipha!'

We seldom ate 'the breakfast' at home any more. Men of high and low degree, whose households I had never visited, engaged me to take *fatoor* with their families. Well before the Call we would accompany our host to his dwelling. In a room apart the men would sit, cigarettes poised, waiting for the signal. In readiness on a low table were mugs of water, flagons of scented syrup and plates of sweet cakes. But oh, the bustle, the fun and the excitement of the kitchen! Fire-pots of all sizes cluttered the stone floor and the women moved among them, stirring, seasoning, tasting judicially and spitting out—for even an accidental swallow discredits the strictest fast. As the moment approached cries of *'Feesa, Feesa!'* accelerated the activity and, by some intuitive timing, at the very instant that the carillon of voices released the Faithful, deep basins were being filled with thick soups, usually of fish, with *bezéen*, the steamed white meal covered with a rich green sauce and lumps of camel meat. Then the *merga*, or vegetable stews with meat, and *shashuka*, the vegetable stews without meat. But the principal dish—the dish upon which the excellence of the whole meal depended was, of course, *cous-cous*—hot as brimstone, heaped high with chicken or lamb, raisins and almonds, or assorted vegetables. Before I joined the menfolk I must break my fast with the women who crouched plying, coaxing, feeding me as if I had been a baby unsure of the way to my mouth! First a raw egg drunk from the shell, then a goblet of orange juice and rose-water sipped slowly, and afterward a savoury morsel of this and that to pique the appetite and 'warn the stomach.'

The Hôtel de Sfax was doing an unparalleled business this Ramadan. All winter it had been very quiet. Occasionally a bedouin would rent a room for a night, but there would be long stretches when Ali and I were the only occupants. One morning during the first week in Ramadan I awoke to a gabble of voices, shrill laughter and the glassy clack-clack of clogs outside in the corridor. While I slept the hotel had undergone some strange metamorphosis. I dressed quickly and looked out. All the doors stood open and a whole sorority of painted women moved familiarly from room to room. They glanced up as I opened my door, 'Bonjour, Madame,' they said respectfully. It was they who had been here all along, it seemed; I was the newcomer, old Rip come down from the mountain. A little dazed, I gave them good morning and withdrew to ponder the enigma. They looked like women from The Street of the Courtesans—their exotic make-up and garments, their voluptuous gait, their insouciance in such a place as this where at any moment a man might appear. My surmise was strengthened by the arrival of the postman for, opening at his knock, I saw that they had not troubled to veil their faces.

I was reading my mail when I heard Kalipha's voice raised in anger below. It was not yet eight o'clock and ordinarily during The Month of Abstinence he never got up until noon, yet here he was bawling out poor Ali who kept insisting 'I do not know, Sidi! I swear—as Mohammed is the Prophet of Allah—I do not know.' Still cursing, Kalipha came on up the stairs.

There was a great clatter of clogs as the women swarmed to receive him, to pelt him with hilarious greetings. Plainly, he was no stranger to them! However, he did not linger in their embraces. There was a peremptory knock at my door. He burst in and locked it behind him. His face was several shades darker, his chest heaved, and the vein on his brow that, barometer-wise, always registered a storm, seemed about to burst. 'Do you realize,' he demanded hoarsely, 'that this hotel has become a nest of harlots? The place is swarming, infested. In Beatrice's room, alone, there are four beds. It is like this that he respects me, Kalipha ben Kassem!' he pounded his breast. 'This is the manner in which he honours a demoiselle who is for two years *Sima Ramadan*! This is the gratitude I get for installing my friends in his dirty bug-ridden hole! Ah, yes, Sidi Tahar,' Kalipha leered, rocking his head from side to side, 'with your savant's turban, your gold-headed cane and your *grande manière du Bey*, you are— you are. . .' he strode to the window, 'a snake!' He spat resoundingly.

It was some time before I could get him quiet enough to explain— between abusive epithets such as 'Pig!' 'Dog!' etc.—that the women were performers from the restaurant below to be quartered here during Ramadan. Some of Kalipha's friends, who felt that he should know the situation, had roused him at cock-crow. His anger had carried him, characteristically, direct to Sidi Tahar. By his own account he had raved like a maniac, and the patron had promised 'by the most great name, by the seal of Solomon and all the rest' that, as soon as certain rooms in the other hotel were vacated, the offenders would be removed there *en masse*.

'Then for the love of God,' I cried, 'why are you carrying on like this! You have Sidi Tahar's word of honour. In the meantime, the women have their place, and I have mine.'

'"Word of honour!"' groaned Kalipha, burying his face in his hands. 'And the French' he demanded with blood-shot eyes, 'have you thought of the French? They distrust you now for living alone in the Arab quarter, for associating with me, "the brother of a murderer." But when it is known that you are living in a bawdy house, not even the President of the United States can clear your reputation. *"Je m'en fiche!"* you can say of yourself, my little one, but what of me? If today I am a "blackguard" and a "villain," isn't it possible that tomorrow I shall be a dangerous criminal?' I recognized the force of this last argument. It was, unfortunately, perfectly possible. 'What do you want me to do?' I asked, for it was patent that something was expected of me.

This was his plan. I was to go at once to Sidi Tahar and in a terrible rage demand that he respect my virtue. Since I could speak very little Arabic, and Tahar no French, I would have to depend mostly upon histrionics—shouts, tears, and threats of moving, winding up with an abrupt, sensational departure. It was Kalipha's conviction that the patron, who had ever known me as a mild, modest young woman, could not fail to be impressed by such an exhibition.

My heart was not in the rehearsal. I had nothing against these women; moreover, Sidi Tahar had always been the kindest landlord. Once, when I had fallen behind in my rent, he had sent word to me that I was not to worry—if my money came, I could pay, but if it did not come, I was his honoured guest for as long as I remained. His wife, Zorrah, and his daughter were my friends; twice already this Ramadan I had broken the fast with them. There was not a house in Kairouan that I entered with more pleasure. Then, too, I had no capacity for anger of this sort—neither was I much of an actress.

I heartily wished myself dead as I marched with Kalipha down the street and up the narrow staircase of the Hôtel Zongbar. Sidi Tahar sat, as usual, cross-legged upon the counter, his immaculate burnous hanging from his shoulders and piled in soft folds about him. His grave eyes shone with a welcoming light and my heart melted as he gestured towards the chairs but, catching Kalipha's stern eye, I recalled my outraged virtue and remained standing. 'Ramadan enforces inhospitality upon me,' he deplored, 'I cannot offer you coffee. But there is no need to apologize to Mademoiselle,' he smiled, 'it is widely known that she is *Sima Ramadan*.' His pleasantry—I had never heard him utter so many words at once—was received with such frigidity that Sidi Tahar looked from one to the other of us in mild astonishment. How should I start? My fingers grasping the folds of my burnous had begun to tremble. Kalipha was staring straight ahead—I could get no help from him. 'I find I have been greatly mistaken in you, Sidi Tahar,' I began a little breathlessly. 'I had thought that you respected me as *nusafir*, as an honest woman, if not *Sima Ramadan*, but it seems I was deceived.' I realized despairingly that my voice wasn't half loud enough. A child could have seen that I wasn't really angry. I began pacing up and down and, all at once, unaccountably, I felt marvellously in command of my rôle of virago. It was as if my tongue had been oiled! Now in English, now in execrable French, I harangued—with all the Arab words I knew thrown in for good measure. I swept back and forth, my eyes I pictured simply blazing, arms flashing out of my burnous to adjure and beat my breast. My volubility and the noise I was making amazed me. Tahar's brothers and clients had come into the room and the consciousness of this marvelling audience brought out in me a talent for fury that none of us thought I possessed. I had just about convinced myself that I had missed my calling, when I caught Sidi Tahar's eye. In it was a kindly, faint, but unmistakable twinkle, whereupon to cover my shame and confusion I swept, with as much majesty as I could muster, down the stairs.

Kalipha shambled after me a moment later. 'But my little one!' he cried with the pride of a tutor whose student has carried off high honours. 'It was magnificent! Before you had reached the street Tahar gave orders that rooms should be prepared. *C'était une victoire superbe, je vous dis! Superbe!'*

'Leave me alone!' I choked from the depth of my remorse.

As for my 'superb victory' it was no victory at all. When after three days the women were still there, even Kalipha had to acknowledge that he had accomplished nothing—except to make a monkey of me. But that he would never acknowledge! I had done magnificently in any case, and was it our fault that Tahar was the father of all pigs?

If Kalipha had been allowed his way I would have moved on the spot. But it was already March, and in May I planned to join friends in Brittany where I would spend a part of the summer. (Beatrice had, by this time, returned to America.) To rent a small house, as he suggested, meant a considerable outlay which, in view of my trip, I simply could not afford. Ramadan would soon be over, the girls would go back to Tunis and Gafsa, Gabes and Sousse, and the Hôtel de Sfax would be itself again. Kalipha dared not be at all vehement on the subject. For days after the now celebrated interview, I could not treat him civilly. At his house I chatted with Mohammed, Eltifa, with everybody but Kalipha. When, as was his custom, he dropped in during the day to find how I was faring, I went on with my work, taking no notice whatsoever of his dejected presence. At last, getting up he would say, very gently: 'Have you letters for the post, *ma petite?'*

'No, thank you.'

'Can I refill the carafe?'

'No, Ali has already done so.'

'Would a morsel of fish delight Kiddypussy?'

'No—yes, well, do as you wish.'

Stung, bewildered, even the will to get me out of my environment was not so strong as the necessity to win me back to our old habit of friendship. But every expression of his solicitude met with the coolest indifference. Until Ramadan was over my high-handed Kalipha was to be kept precisely where I had him—under my thumb.

Meanwhile, it was a strange experience to be living, inviolate, in the midst of a whore-house. The artistes, who had been picked from the restricted districts of cities all over the dominion, were under as strict surveillance as if they had been lodged on The Street; by law they were prohibited from quitting the premises. During the day things were fairly quiet. They slept late, then trailed about in *négligés* laughing, jabbering, kidding Ali, squabbling and rapturously hailing Kalipha and the postman. Quite often they had fights—wild, primitive bouts that simply terrified me. Once something very large crashed against my door—I think it was a wash-bowl. Their shouts and screams brought half the street rushing up to quell the riot, but five minutes after such a contest they were, to all appearances, the best of friends.

They always treated me with a kind of shy formality. As I came and went it was always, *'Bonjour, Madame,'* nothing more. Only once did one of them knock at my door. She had in her hand a sheet of ruled paper and an envelope. She had heard my writing-machine, she explained hesitantly, in perfectly intelligible French. Was I, perhaps, a writer? In that case, would I—would I have the great kindness to write her mother a letter? Why of course, would she come in? I took her paper and picked up my pen. But maybe she preferred me to use the typewriter? She brightened. O would I! It would be so much more—so much more chic. *'Chère Maman,'* she dictated, *'Je suis bien. Je n'ai plus du mal à la tête. Je suis à Kairouan avec un café-concert. Il ne faut pas faire le mauvais sang pour moi. Je suis toute à vous. Klarah Galeenie.'* While I was addressing the envelope, she took a pencil and below the typed signature made her own mark, explaining, 'Like that, *Ummi* will see it is me.'

Towards sundown every evening the girls began to prepare their *fatoor*, for they were keeping the fast as scrupulously as the rest of us. Each had her own fire-pot, her own earthen vessels, and the picture they made grouped together at the far end of the hall, stooping and crouching in their brilliant head-dresses and hip-scarves, was memorably beautiful.

The 'concert' in the back room of the restaurant began early and went on until midnight. When it ended below stairs, its sequel started above, and until daybreak the Hôtel de Sfax gave itself up to carousal—doors banging, mandolines, hilarious laughter, coffee boys running up and down stairs, singing, the constant throb of pottery drums, clapping, lusty shouts of 'Sahit! Sahit!'—as one of the hostesses did a hot dance—clients coming and clients going to make room for more!

After the *sahoor*, our last meal, when Kalipha, very reluctantly, took me home, the revelry was still going on, but behind closed doors, doubtlessly out of deference to Madame. Occasionally on the dim stairs we would meet a young man of good family; Kalipha would avert his eyes as the other slipped hastily past us. In such circumstances, one must never, never mortify a man by recognition.

My new attitude towards Kalipha was becoming increasingly hard to maintain. Once I began to see the humour of my command performance, angry resentment was done for, and all the affection I felt for my friend surged back with increase because I now knew him better. It was my little cat, of whom we were both absurdly fond, that made it hardest to hold out against Kalipha's blandishments.

Like all the black cats I have ever known, Kiddypussy was an out and out individualist, and, like any cat that is made much of, he was articulate and knowing. 'He talks. I swear he talks!' Kalipha often marvelled. His own household had always included a couple of furtive, half-wild, negligible felines, but never had he known the like of this one! *'Mais vous savez, il n'est pas un chat!'* he would solemnly assure me. In short, Kiddypussy was in a fair way of becoming legendary among the Arabs who were perfectly ready to believe him to be three parts djinn.

It was on a morning toward the middle of Ramadan that Kalipha came in with boiled liver. I greeted him briefly and turned back to my work. He waited in silence until Kiddypussy had polished the plate. 'Was the liver to your taste, my little monsieur?' he demanded. 'Tell me, have you eaten well? Eaten until the stomach is round like a melon? Dined, in effect, like a prince?' He kept this up until the cat left off washing his face and threw his whole weight against Kalipha's leg. 'Ah, that is better!' he said approvingly, gathering him to his lap. 'For whether you have eaten well or badly, my friend, politeness is the principal thing in the life. And now, give me your ear for a little moment. Sit down, that is right, and listen well, if you please, for my heart is heavy, heavy, Kiddypussy, and who have I but you to tell of my misery?'

The understanding between the two was uncanny! From the tail of my eye I saw that the cat had obediently settled himself and had assumed, under the even strokes of the brown hand, quite a meditative air.

'I assure you, my friend,' Kalipha continued, 'I walk about like a man condemned. Abdallah, Eltifa, they speak to me, I do not hear. "His thoughts are on pilgrimage," they say. Ah, yes, they know my despair! I walk, I sit, I make my little purchases, I prepare the *fatoor*, but always it is as if somebody else were wearing these garments, this robe, this vest, this fez. This morning, while I was marketing, you understand, I stepped in front of a camel—a camel high as a minaret—enormous—a veritable *chameau de bataille*, I assure you. They seized me by the skirts not a second too soon! But whether I live or die, Kiddypussy, it is all the same to me. Will you visit me sometimes at Sidi Abdelli? I shall be sleeping beneath the cold earth. . .' A few minutes more of this and I had either to laugh or to cry, so I laughed, we both laughed, and Kiddypussy, as if he perfectly understood, jumped from Kalipha's lap into mine!

Oh the relief of being friends again! Reconciled, without any mention of moving,—decidedly, we had both triumphed! I had not long, however, to cherish this illusion. Two days after our reconciliation, quite early in the morning, there was a knock at the door and Kalipha came in followed by his friend Sidi Brahim, a *spahis* or policeman, and Sidi Sallah, Tahar's half-brother who ran the restaurant downstairs. All three had the look of bringing me very bad news. '*Ma pauvre petite*,' Kalipha sighed as he seated himself, 'you did not close your eyes all night!'

'But I slept very well!' I said, truthfully.

'Impossible!' they cried out aghast. I had not been molested? Nobody had tried my door? I had not heard? The fighting? The screams? Not even the shots? Why, between three and four, this place was a madhouse! Jealous clients doing battle up and down the corridor—the women tearing around, hanging out of the windows screeching for help— a mob on the stairs! The revolver shots were heard in the French town!

Up to this point they had all talked at once. 'Unhappily,' went on Sidi Brahim very gravely, 'Monsieur the commissaire has heard of the *scandale*. But what would you, he is not deaf! This morning I was summoned before him and— and—but it is necessary that I tell you the truth—I was charged with the responsibility of moving you to safer lodgings. You will pardon me, Mademoiselle, I do only my duty which, Allah in His wisdom knows, is utterly detestable to me! Permit me to counsel you, Mademoiselle,' he lowered his eyes apologetically, 'it would be wise to move at once.'

'At once !' I cried, 'this minute? But where shall I go!'

'I assure you from my heart,' soothed Kalipha, taking my hand, 'there is absolutely no cause for anxiety. Your good friends have settled everything. Sidi Brahim,' he put his hand on the other's shoulder, 'came directly to me. "The situation is such-and-such" said he "what can we do?" Oh, I tell you, Sherifa, he was distracted! So together we found you a house. Indeed, we have already persuaded the landlord—Sidi Taïb who has his shop in the saddle *souk*—to waive the quarter lease and allow you to pay by the month. As for furniture—Sallah, here, has already laid the situation before Sidi Tahar who has said you may have the use of everything in this room, without charge, for as long as you need them. Tell me, am I right or wrong, Sidi Sallah?' (Sallah smilingly swore he was right.) 'So, my little one,' Kalipha declared, 'all you have to do is put Kiddypussy in this bag and stroll over to your new home. And what a beautiful little house it is! You will see—*un vrai chateau!*' His effusion was put an end to by a loud knocking and Ali stuck his head in to say that the donkey awaited below. 'Then come, let us go!' Kalipha cried gaily, whereupon, in the same spirit, they all fell to carrying out my table, bed, chairs, and wash-stand. Within an hour I was moved.

FATMA BECOMES A PROBLEM

I suppose I would have disliked any house I had moved into under the same circumstances, even if it had been a 'château,' which mine assuredly was not. It was the typical lower-class house, a hollow square of one storey situated in a foul little lane solid with dwellings more or less like mine. On the stone lintel were graven the Arabic characters, 'He is the Great Creator, the Everlasting.' How many centuries of tenants had these charmed words protected and reminded of mortality! The door-key (it looked capable of opening a dungeon) admitted you into a vaulted passage which crooked into the court. Opening upon the court, at right angles to each other, were two long narrow rooms, each having a pair of low windows, one on either side the door. There was, also, a dark, rank-smelling crypt, a combination kitchen-latrine with a brick oven and a simple hole in the floor.

'Isn't it nice?' cried Kalipha with anxious exuberance as I stood looking around. 'Here, you see, is the well. Water for cleaning and washing only. Did you remark that the rooms have been freshly whitewashed? How the good sun pours into this little court! It is charming, isn't it? Well-arranged and so clean. Perfect, in fact, for a demoiselle living alone. Ah, look up, *ma petite*, your neighbours have come to bid you welcome!' Several kerchiefed heads were poised upon the parapet. Without glancing up, Kalipha spoke to them, and immediately their fingers flew to their mouths and the *zaghareet* crowned us. 'They are wishing you good fortune! Thank them, my little one! Tell them *katarheerick!*'

But my thoughts were morbidly measuring the height of the walls. The parapet was scarcely twelve feet above us; in the black of night a man could easily lower himself into the court. I was suddenly belligerent. I had been compelled to move—actually or by connivance I would never know—but not Kalipha nor Sidi Brahim nor even the French could force me to live here alone. Kalipha was prepared for everything. 'What an idea!' he exclaimed reproachfully. 'Do you think I would permit you to live here alone! I, who am responsible for your peace of mind and safety! Ah, *ma petite*, for shame! At this very moment Fatma and the rest of my effects are on the way. Look!' he pointed, 'there is your chamber—and here is mine. Quite separate, quite private. But come now, to work! First we must burn benjoin upon the fire-pot—disinfect this house of evil djinns that would make us mischief!'

One small donkey sufficed to transfer Kalipha's chattels and that evening, by way of housewarming, he prepared an elaborate *fatoor* in our own court. Eltifa and Abdallah were invited and, to Kalipha's evident satisfaction, Abdallah completed the fumigation of our dwelling by chanting the ninety-nine names of Allah. One could fairly see the djinns scrambling out of cracks and cornersfalling over one another—darting every way—running for their lives at the sound of those august attributes! 'Now,' sighed Kalipha with immense relief, 'the house is habitable!'

The excitement of moving soon wore away, but the strangeness of my new quarters never did. I felt I was buried alive. In exchange for my window, the terrace, I had a square blue patch of sky. I missed the torrential noise of the street, that full exhilarating sense of living in the very core of Kairouan. Fatma and I were alone much of the day and the house was dead quiet, so quiet I could hear the rapid whiff-whiff of the fan whenever she lit the fire-pot. My table had been set near the window, for although the court always blazed with sunshine, my room was as dim as one of the mosque-tombs that dot the cemeteries. I was never unconscious of the room. Uneasy, faintly depressed, I was always secretly relieved when the evening brought us together in Kalipha's lamp-lit chamber. Most of the time I went through only the motions of work, but occasionally, when I was really absorbed, lost to my surroundings, a hideous fright would grab hold of me—a feeling that someone, something, had come up behind me. 'What is the matter?' Fatma would look up with her quizzical smile as I burst into the court. But I couldn't explain the seizure even to myself. Perhaps I was tired, my nerves were ravelled, I needed a change. I knew that I was very worried. For Fatma was ill, dreadfully ill, and there was nothing I could do about it.

My pleas on her behalf had always angered Kalipha, nevertheless he had tolerated her for my sake. The beginning of the end came last winter. His worry over Kadeja's trouble had told on his temper and poor Fatma, it often seemed, had only to set a vessel here instead of there to demonize him. Frequently when I came in to dinner, Fatma was not in sight. The explanation was invariably the same. There had been a row, Kalipha had beaten her or not beaten her, as the case might be, and Fatma was moping in the dark clammy hole off the court known as 'the storage room.' It was Eltifa and Abdallah's policy at such times to keep strictly to themselves. Mohammed, who had no love for his stepmother, was always as furious as Kalipha, and so, despite daily-renewed vows to mind my own business, I always found myself championing Fatma.

The climax came one miserable night during the rainy season. Fatma had a heavy cold which I was doctoring with aspirin and goose-grease. In reply to my 'How is Fatma this evening?' Mohammed shrugged his shoulders in the direction of the storage room. The rain was beating into the court. I threw my burnous over my head and dashed across to the threshold of the void where Fatma was hiding. To the point of tears I beseeched her to come back to the fire, but it was of no use, she would not even answer. My dismay, the fact that I could eat no supper, only made matters worse, for Kalipha's anger, which had cooled by the time I arrived, was rapidly regaining the boiling point. Getting up suddenly, he flung open the door and commanded Fatma once, twice to return. Then, receiving no answer, to my horror he started after her with his cane. From that black cavern I heard her cry imploringly, *'Mreetha, y'Sidi, mreetha!'* I am sick, O my master! I am sick! My own shrieks spared her a beating, but Kalipha returned with dreadful decision, hurled down the stick, and threw his burnous over his head. He started out, then paused, his hand upon the door. 'It is finished! To-morrow I divorce her. I am now—*Silence!'* he glared as I opened my mouth, 'I am now going to give her sister warning. I will divorce this woman, but I shall not turn her out like a dog, as better men than I would do. No! I will first warn her sister, her uncle, that between them they can decide where she is to go.' The door banged behind him as he flung himself into the rain.

That Kalipha may not seem an utter brute, it is only fair to present his side of the story. In matrimony he had never been lucky. His first wife, Aisha, fought with his family. His second, Shelbeia, disgraced her husband by flirting to and from the baths. (But she parted her veils once too often!) Hanoona, the mother of Mohammed, neglected house and child and, on the day he fell down the stairs, Kalipha announced that he was finished with women ... as wives.

He kept his vow for three years, or, until Eltifa rebelled. Against every argument of hers he could stand firm, except this, 'Keep your vow, O my brother. Nobody has a better right. But marry yourself a servant. Among the women stranded by divorce you will find many that would be thankful to earn their keep in wedlock.' So he was forced to relent; it was noised about town that Kalipha ben Kassem was in the market for a 'wife.'

Now Fatma had reached the marriageable age when the death of her parents forced her to live with her sister, a shrewish woman, many years older than Fatma, with a raft of children and a surly husband who had all he could do to feed his own. Fatma became the family drudge. Food and house-room were begrudged her. The sister's one idea was to marry her off. But the girl had no dowry, no talent whatsoever for weaving (unpardonable shortcoming in Kairouan), and, besides virginity, little else to recommend her. Nevertheless, a husband was found for her. Fatma was married, but soon divorced. She could not return to her sister's. Her only other relative was an elderly uncle, Hassein ben Ali, who was probably the most unhappy polygamist in Kairouan and the butt of all jokes on the subject. Reluctantly, to save his niece from The Street, he took her in.

He was among the first to button-hole Kalipha. And if he swore that his niece was a model of thrift, neatness and industry, an inestimable asset, a complete angel, nobody could seriously blame him. Certainly Kalipha never did. In marriage you took your chance. You stuck your hand in the grab-bag and pulled out—if Allah willed—a Kadeja or a Zinibe. What Kalipha got was Fatma.

Poor Fatma succeeded as a servant no better than a wife. Not only could she neither cook nor weave, she proved unteachable and lazy. She was, also, an incurable slattern. Folded away in the painted chest were hip-scarves, pantaloons, and headkerchiefs that Kalipha had bought for her from time to time, yet nothing short of violence would induce her to change her garments. Her drab, loveless existence was enlivened only by such excitement as she could make for herself. It was discovered, for instance, some time after her coming, that food of both households had a way of disappearing. The cats were blamed until the day Eltifa caught her sister-in-law in the act of tying a basin of *cous-cous* to a cord dangling into the court. There was a frightful uproar, Fatma was never again detected in her philanthropy, but food continued to vanish.

On the other hand, she had her own little system of economy. Kalipha's fortunes fluctuated from day to day. If he had been lucky enough to 'trap a tourist,' and had twenty francs in his pocket, he was rich. He spent lavishly, splendidly, but the next day he might be destitute. Then it was that Fatma would quietly take from her little hoard whatever he required. Was it cigarettes? She would put into his hand the half-dozen she had filched from him last week. Was it charcoal, tomato-paste or meal? This ant-like practice simply delighted Kalipha. 'O djinneyeh!' he would petition the air, his eyes twinkling, 'grant me, if you please, a garlic for the evening's macaroni!' And Fatma would eventually appear and, with a mocking little smile, hold out to him the garlic.

But one swallow does not make a summer, nor did this single trait reconcile Kalipha to her ignorance and sloth. I could not but feel that if he could secure her a certain refuge, I had no longer any right to keep him from divorcing her.

After that night Fatma's cold grew steadily worse. She would not keep to her bed, but dragged herself around, wasting and coughing until she was beyond the aid of my aspirin tablets. Nobody paid particular attention to her, and, even if he had had the money, Kalipha would not hear of calling in the doctor.

Meanwhile, he was finding it no easy matter to dispose of his wife. Her sister's door, he soon found, was shut to her—slammed and locked. For all she cared, Fatma could die on the doorstep. So the pursuit of her uncle began. It really doesn't seem possible that in a town the size of Kairouan it would take weeks to find a man! Kalipha waited hours in Hassein's favourite coffee-house, hung about the mosque of his devotions, haunted the quarter in which he lived—to no purpose.

One fine moonlit night, just after I moved, we were strolling along the main street when we bumped into him. At a word from Kalipha he took leave of his companions and we seated ourselves on a bench beneath the pepper trees near the Djeladin Gate and Kalipha ordered coffees. Contrary to my expectations, Sidi Hassein was a stern-faced majestic old gentleman, not at all the sort, one would say, to be husbanding three harpies. The salutations were endless. One as much as the other was on tenterhooks, yet the leisurely tide of 'How is your health? How is your household? Are you well? Is nothing wrong with you?' droned on and on, until when they got to their respective cousins' children, I could listen no longer. When I awoke Sidi Hassein was taking his leave. He swept away and I asked, 'Well, what did he say?' Nervously, Kalipha lit a cigarette. 'What could he say? He will take her back. Only,' it was a few moments before he completed the sentence, 'this evening I learned that Fatma's mother died of tuberculosis.'

There was a noticeable improvement in his attitude toward Fatma after that; it was as if he was aware for the first time that she was mortal. Sidi Hassein would relieve him of Fatma tomorrow, but now the thought of losing her among those termagants was horrible to him. Whether from fear of her disease or genuine concern for her welfare, he tried desperately to get her into the free ward of the hospital. He was told that only paupers were eligible and, so long as Fatma had a husband, she could not be considered destitute. For the time being, while she was with me, she was getting milk, rest, and sunshine, but what would become of her after I left? It was this worry that unstrung me, persecuted me with the mysterious terror that made me fear I might be losing my mind. This fear, itself, must have driven me mad if I hadn't found—to my unspeakable relief—that all along Kalipha himself had been the prey of the same gruesome sensations! He, however, did not attribute it to our anxiety. 'It is this house.' he said with a shudder. 'It is polluted, it breeds evil. Though I said nothing, I felt it from the first. Somebody must be interred beneath the pavement. If a house is haunted, neither benjoin nor the ninety-nine names of Allah can purify it.'

Finally, after much deliberation and discussion, Kalipha arrived at this plan. On the day of my departure he would divorce Fatma, thus enabling her to get into the hospital. Next, with the sole object of stabilizing his resources, he would marry himself a weaver. If Fatma came out of the hospital alive, he could then afford to provide for her. The plan sounded all right, but would it work? Kalipha hadn't a doubt in the world. He even explained it all to Fatma and readily obtained her consent. To be well again, poor girl, that was her one desperate hope!

Her problem settled, Kalipha began, with Eltifa's able assistance, to cast about for another wife. Never since I had known him had there been any confusion in his mind about the type. 'She need not be young,' he elaborated. 'Youth—*phu*—I've had enough of it! She need not be beautiful—for if she be beautiful her value may reside only in her face. She must be a widow or a *divorcée* for they are acquainted with life—and they come cheaper. Let her be calm, clean, and thrifty—I do not demand much. But, most important of all, she must weave!'

The time for finding a gem of this description was short, because in two weeks I was to leave, and Kalipha was very anxious that I pass judgment upon his intended. There were three candidates for his bed. At the offset they were all 'gazelles,' but, upon closer investigation, two were eliminated. Of the third, Turkia daughter of Sadoc, Eltifa had great hopes. I was urged to accompany her when she called upon the girl's family to inquire into her qualifications. So one afternoon, a few days before my departure, I set out with Eltifa and Halima, her closest friend and the chief of her orchestra.

I was ready to be charmed with Turkia. First of all, she was not a *divorcée*, but a widow who had been married to the same husband fifteen years. Secondly, her name was favourably known among the local rug merchants. Upon her husband's death, she had returned to the home of her parents who were having a little difficulty marrying her off again on account of her age—she was over thirty.

We were received by the women of the family as ordinary visitors, although, of course, the object of our call was clearly understood. Turkia was present, but her mother and sisters-in-law did all the talking. The conversation was easy and affable, while Turkia served us coffee and little date-stuffed cakes—of her own making we were told. For my part I liked her immediately, and I tried to tell her so when our eyes met. She looked so trustworthy, so wholesome and capable! She was not young, but certainly she wasn't old; she wasn't beautiful, but she was far from being ugly. She could cook; she could weave—that carpet on the loom was hers. What a wife for Kalipha! I only feared she was *too* good for him !

I could hardly wait to learn Eltifa's opinion. 'Well, Sherifa,' she began, as, our visit over, we moved off down the lane, 'What do you think of her?' My eager praise caused her to chuckle under her veil. 'Ah, yes,' she sighed, 'if my brother is not a dunce he will snatch this ruby!'

'O Eltifa, he will!' I cried. 'She is all that he asks of a woman!'

A dry little laugh was her answer.

I went directly home with her for it had been arranged that Kalipha would be waiting for us there. He and Abdallah were drinking tea when we came in. Dispassionately, Eltifa delivered herself of her report as she slowly unwound her *haïk*. When she had done, I began. Unlike Eltifa, I could not contain my enthusiasm, and they all started laughing. Even Abdallah's sober face shone like a jack-o'-lantern. 'You are a born match-maker!' Kalipha kept crying until I began to feel that he was much more amused than interested. Finally, I reproached him. 'But, *ma petite!*' he cried virtuously, 'How can you say that! I am listening, I am impressed. Continue! She is about thirty you say, rather plain-looking—go on!'

'But, as you yourself have said,' I insisted, 'these things are not important. For she can cook and weave and. . .' Here I caught Kalipha smiling broadly across at Abdallah. Exasperated, I asked him point-blank. 'Will you take her for your wife?'

'Why of course, my little one!' he declared, straightening his face with difficulty. This Turkia bint Sadoc is the one wife for me. My search is at an end!' But it was of no use—he couldn't keep back his laughter. 'What a little match-maker!' he gasped through his fingers.

THE ADORNING OF
THE BRIDE

It was incredible that a short journey by sea and land could take one so far, far away. Kairouan—Concarneau—were ever two cities more strongly contrasted? Swift-moving skies, air like brine, steep streets, crowded harbour, coifs, sabots, peasants—grim and self-contained, one could fancy almost inimical: that was Concarneau. It stimulated, it invigorated me, but it could never endear itself to me as Kairouan had done.

I had not long to wait for Kalipha's first letter, written in the flourishing penmanship of the public scribe. Its contents should have been no great surprise: 'At last my sister has found me a wife! You well remember the nice little man, Sidi Mohammed, who shines shoes in the *souks*? This Kadusha is his stepdaughter. She is a virgin, very young, they tell me, and brown as a date. I like very much a brown skin. It is certain that Sherifa will love her! The marriage contract has already been signed, and I await only your return for the ceremony.'

So this was the result of our pains! Turkia's talents, her long successful career as a wife—these things did not count. Nothing counted, in reality, except virginity—virginity and a brown skin! The patience, the sympathy I had wasted upon his bombastic tirades! Eltifa's weary laugh came back to me; long ago *she* had learned. Well, he had doubtless got what he deserved—some silly little thing, all face and figure, of whom he would soon tire. His casual assumption that I would return for the marriage irritated me, but what really angered me was the fact that he had not even mentioned Fatma. She had evidently been divorced, if the contract had been signed, but was she in the hospital? I had not the patience for the hyperbolical congratulations that Kalipha fondly expected. In one scant sentence I wished him well. The rest of my letter was devoted to urgent inquiries after Fatma.

Three weeks must have passed before I received his classic answer. 'My dear sister, I am well, but my pocket-book is sick. That is to say, empty. First, there was the expense of buying the new wife. Then, during the fête my distinguished nephew from Salambo, with two of his friends, passed five days with me. This cost me dear, I assure you. Then Fatma died—another little expense. It was a great pity that you were not here for the birthday of our glorious Prophet.'

'*Fatma est morte—encore une petite dépense.*' No more than that. The mail was distributed as I was eating breakfast and I remember that, long after the dining-room was cleared, I sat there holding my letter, looking off to sea in the direction of Kairouan, trying to realize that Fatma was dead. I could search the White City over and I would not find the unfathomable little creature. That she was dead, at an expense to Kalipha, was all that I knew, all that I would learn from correspondence. *Fatma est morte—encore une petite dépense!* I could not get the words out of my mind. For days they swung in time to my movements, my conversation; at night they paced sombrely through my sleep. Fatma was everywhere, enigmatically smiling at me from the *paysage* across the harbour, from among the painted sails, the clouds in the sky. It was never the plump, tousled-headed little creature who had first welcomed us to Kalipha's household, but a tiny wraith with dervish hair. The sea murmured *Fatma est morte—encore une petite dépense*, the wind took it up. And sometimes at night I heard them both moaning, *Mreetha y'Sidi! Mreetha!*

There had been tears in her eyes when we said good-bye that morning in the court. 'You will get well, Fatma,' I told her. 'The hospital will cure you.'

'*Inshallah,*' she had smiled mistily. As Allah wills. I think she knew that she would not get any better.

I could not be interested in this Kadusha. I supposed I would try to like her for Kalipha's sake, but for the attempt even, I needed time. I advised him repeatedly not to postpone the wedding on my account, yet his letters continued to assure me that the nuptials attended my return. So, as a sort of memorial to Fatma, or perhaps from innate perversity, I changed the date of my sailing and returned three weeks later than I had intended.

Kalipha was at the dock to meet us. As I stood near the bulwark scanning the crowd on the shore with eyes made clear and critical by absence, I spotted him with something like horror. Good God! I thought. Is that black diabolical-looking Arab, that hideous caricature of a villain, your friend! He was alternately wiping his eyes with and waving a large red and yellow handkerchief. It was only five days to his wedding, yet no man had ever looked less the bridegroom. He was unkempt, unshaven, and wearing what appeared to be a child's white burnous. (Afterwards I learned that, having sold his own burnous for the price of the fare to Tunis, he had borrowed Abdallah's for the journey and his dishevelment was due to the fact that he had spent the night on the wharves.)

His vociferous joy, my own happiness to be back, soon swept all that was unworthy and strange from my feelings and, by the time we were settled *vis-à-vis* in the train for Kairouan, I was seeing him in the old way—a lovable mixture of watchdog, father, brother, and child.

Now, as we rolled across Tunisian country, I heard the whole story of Fatma. If it was grim, it was, also, mercifully short. She was admitted into the hospital on the same day that she was divorced, and on the next, Kalipha, with an easy mind, took the family to Monastir, a village on the coast where they spent a fortnight with Jannat's schoolmaster son Mohammed. Fatma was dead and buried by the time he returned. His account of her end, consequently, was patched together from hearsay.

Fatma was in the hospital less than a week. She was always stealing things, it seems. From the moment she entered, the ward was demoralized; the doctors went crazy trying to enforce order and quiet. Finally, when she was caught stealing biscuits from the patient alongside of her, *'ils la jettent la porte.'* The hospital is located about a mile from the city and it is a fact that early one morning some bedouins found Fatma lying by the road. They carried her with them to Kairouan and, after trying the sister, they left her at the Uncle's. The very next day the women put her out. She went from door to door after that, 'but everybody feared her disease.' So she crept into a mosque where she was found insensible and sent back to the hospital. 'It was several days before she could die, the poor thing. They said she was like a finger.' She was buried, without funeral, in the cemetery of Sidi Arfah. That was all, except that her clothes—pretty things folded like new—reverted to Kalipha.

It is a seven-hour journey by train from Tunis to Kairouan, and, in all that time, Kalipha did not mention his fiancée unless I did, and then indifferently, as 'the new one' or 'this Kadusha.' For fear of embarrassing him, I suppressed most of the questions that had been accumulating during my absence. One, however, simply shot past my guard. 'But Kalipha, how could you *afford* the purchase price of a virgin?'

'It was not high in this case,' he explained placatingly. 'Sidi Mohammed, who is my friend, was willing to let me have the girl at a bargain. She is only his stepdaughter, you know, and he has two children—and another *en route*. Two hundred francs is cheap for a virgin, but it was riches to Sidi Mohammed, poor man.' There was quite a pause. 'You know,' he added self-consciously, 'this Kadusha can weave. They say she is very strong at the loom. A veritable tigress, they say.' As I gave no sign of being the least bit impressed, he pursued, 'Demand of the rug merchants. They will tell you the prices her carpets bring. Ask Basheer or Mohammed el Mishri—ask any of them!' I averted my head toward the window. 'Ah, yes,' he reproached me sadly, 'I divine your thoughts. But you will see!'

Kalipha was to take possession of his wife on Thursday, the eve of the Sabbath, and he returned to Kairouan on the preceding Saturday, the second day of the momentous Marriage Week. There was nothing in his behaviour, however, to indicate that this was not just another week to him. I teased him a little about his indifference. 'Oh, yes, you *seem* very calm, but one knows that your heart is jumping. It is not possible for a bridegroom to be calm!'

'*C'est beaucoup possible*,' he sighed with regret. '*Mais qu'est ce que vous voulez? Après beaucoup de marriages—est surtout quand on n'est plus jeune*.' But, whether the groom be young or old, he said, the Marriage Week belongs principally to the bride. Which, of course, is perfectly true. The sheltered girl has lived for this. It is her moment of triumph, debut-and consummation—the very summit of her existence. The strict seclusion in which she was reared is justified; her parents' fondest hope for her is fulfilled. She is *larossa*, virgin bride, theme of lyric odes and romances, the plaint of every popular song. For her the beat of the drums, the *zaghareet*, the festal tapers and incense! For her the ancient honours! Never again in the course of her whole life will there be anything like it. For when the brief period is up, as the property of her husband instead of her father, she will step back into obscurity. She has had woman's full measure of homage; of that sweet meed there will not be one more drop. Even at the birth of her children the praise will not be for her.

125

Continuously, for seven days, the bride's home is filled with women come to celebrate her good fortune and to assist in the beautification of her body. The activity of the musicians and the beauty specialist keep the air glittering with ecstatic joycries. But, like the queen bee in her turbulent hive, the betrothed sits inscrutable amidst the noisy jubilance. Enthroned in her stiff finery she presides—never moving, never speaking, never opening her eyes. Custom has assigned her a heavy rôle for the duration of this week—the personification of Maidenly Modesty. She must not desecrate it by so much, it would seem, as the flicker of a lash.

Each night of the Marriage Week is sacred to its own ritual. On the first, The Night of the Henna, the bride's feet and hands are stained with the virtuous leaf so beloved of the Prophet, on the second, she is conducted to the baths, the third is dedicated to another application of the henna. She is taken, on the fourth evening, once more to the *hammam*. On this occasion the minstrels accompany the bathers, and while she is being washed, shaved, perfumed, and whitened, they sing of the coming event, The Ineffable Entrance. On the fifth night her finger tips and the palms of her hands are blackened with *harcoos*, the sixth is simply the night of farewell. On the afternoon of the seventh day, The Night of the Entrance, she is finally given the traditional make-up and clothed in bridal raiment.

For reasons which have no place in this chapter, I did not see Kalipha's bride until the afternoon of the great day itself. As Mohammed and I were on our way to her home. I discovered that I was really quite excited.

He was none too sure of our direction, but once in the right quarter we had only to follow the sounds of rejoicing that hung like an aureole above the roof-tops causing passers-by to shout, *'Salloo-annebee!'* Bless ye the Prophet! The noise led us into a lane against the ramparts where we located the house by the Marriage Sign—a huge tree of life crudely described in whitewash on that part of the city wall opposite the door.

The little boy had to let the knocker fall sharply several times before it raised a splatter of hurrying pattens. To the accompaniment of the *zaghareet*, I was led into an exotic garden of women with kohled eyes, hennaed feet and hands, and breasts that swelled from tinselled bodices like rising dough. Raw, brilliant colours—as many to each costume as there were pieces of apparel—wove and intermingled in barbaric patterns.

Above, the bright heads of the uninvited garlanded the parapet. A little grandstand of five or six tiers, a customary feature of such occasions, had been erected across one corner of the court, and upon it were seated the elect—young women who had, themselves, been wed within the last year. The splendour, if not the rank, of *larossa* was theirs again to-day, for they were wearing their gold and silver marriage costumes—the sack-like tunics and paunchy trousers of which gave them a chunky appearance suggesting bags of bullion ranged in rows. Their hair flamed uniformly with henna and perched over their ears were incongruous little caps—gilt or pearl-strung, flat or cone-shaped. While of amulets (notably fish and Hands of Fatma) and other jewellery, each wore at least a bushel. These exalted ones took no part in the merrymaking: they were the show-piece. Nobody attempted to distract them from the contemplation of their magnificence. They simply sat, their dyed hands, stiff with rings, one upon the other in their laps, looking benignly down upon the unmarried girls and worn matrons.

In another corner of the spacious court was the familiar ring of black mounds, the musicians. I recognized Eltifa by her heavy gold bracelets, but I could not expect her to greet me today or to be even conscious that I had come in. Bundled guests kept coming, each new group a signal for vocal comets of rejoicing, the uninvited shrilling as generously as the guests themselves. But the real noise was coming from the chamber where the bride was in the hands of the *belláneh*, the beauty specialist. In there, the *zaghareet* was almost continuous, one bright burst succeeding and mingling with another.

Kadusha's gentle-faced mother, Zorrah, who was portly with child, and her mother, a toothless, humorous old woman, had taken kind charge of me from the moment I entered. After I had been served coffee, they undertook the prodigious feat of getting me into the bridal chamber. It was jammed to the threshold, nevertheless I was pushed and propelled until I stood within a finger's length of the bride. She sat with her back against the wall near the low grilled window. Her feet and hands were still tied up in plump moist bags of henna-meal. She looked like a doll with her eyes shut, her legs in lace-edged pantaloons stuck out in front of her, her arms loose at her sides. A *takritah* was snugly bound about her head to protect her hair and a piece of white material, wrapped around her under the arm-pits, served as an apron.

She was young—far too young by western standards to be the wife of Kalipha who, although he did not know his exact age, must have been fifty. Yet, like Arab brides in general, she did not look a child. Her face, her arms, her rich bosom had the fresh ripeness of early womanhood. Her skin was dusky—the *café-crème* her husband hoped it would be—her lips were very full and her closed eyes gave her countenance the usual *larossa* look of great passivity and submission. As if to test her immobility, the women talked at and twitted her, whispered in her ears, asked her mirth-provoking questions, but not a muscle of the quiet face quivered. I searched it over for some clue to her character. The full lips—did they mean that she was petulant or sullen? God forbid! The eyes dark-fringed and far apart, the high cheek bones, that broad, clear brow—what did they signify? The blind docility of her face disarmed me of the little I knew of physiognomy; it was as incomprehensible to me as the moon or a coin kicked up from the dust of Carthage. Her youth and girlish bloom were all that I really saw, and so strong was their appeal that I forgave Kadusha for being a virgin, for not being, frankly, Turkia bint Sadoc! Rockets of praise were shooting up to Allah. Instinctively to one of them I tied the fervent prayer, 'Make her strong to command her husband's respect, and, for her own sake, O great Allah, make her imperturbable!'

Crouched facing her was Hahja Bala, the aged specialist in the decoration of brides. A withered sorceress she seemed with her mysterious pots, vases, and jars, her abracadabra—for as she worked she invoked divine assistance in a kind of keening chant. The women were taking turns rubbing almond lotion into the arms; Hahja Bala was giving all her skill to the face. When it had been creamed and powdered until it was the dead white of chalk, she selected from the little tools in her lap an ivory probe. Dipping this into liquid kohl, with slow calculated strokes she began the ornamentation of the eyes. An Egyptian urn of remote antiquity might have served as a model. The eyebrows were emphasized, stylized; the lashes coaxed together into tiny lacquered spikes; then a thick black line was drawn along the edge of each lid. Now Hahja Bala discarded the probe for a blunt needle. Dipping it, also, into the kohl-vessel she wrought two parallel strips of black lace across the chaste brow. It was not the first to be adorned by those gnarled old fingers! Exquisite arabesques—minutely fashioned of flowers and minarets, crescents, stars, intertwining leaves and pyramided dots—a stately flow from temple to temple. The delight of the onlookers was frantic as Hahja Bala, always crooning, roofed her eyes with her hands to survey her handiwork. With the same sure needle, next, she left here and there, on chin, throat, the slope of each breast, a single delicate motif. Now for the lips. With scarlet she accented their luscious pout. And last of all the cheeks. For them the bright pink salve. She took a wad of it on a forefinger and painted on each side of the face a solid circle of raw cerise. By now Kadusha was absolutely blotted out. Every trace of individuality, of life even, was gone. We were looking at an empty, grotesque mask—the same that Zinibe had worn upon her bier, the same that Lellah Zorrah would wear in a few months when she sat in state upon the natal chair.

Hahja Bala was done. The *zaghareet* published the glad news until it seemed that, wherever he might be, Kalipha ben Kassem must know that the face of his bride was ready for his sight! The meal-bags were taken off, the green paste washed away. Feet and hands were the orange-red of flame, but the toes, the finger-tips, and the palms were black. The apron was removed, her hair unbound. The rented cloth of gold raiment was brought in. At its appearance we all moved excitedly into the open, leaving the final rites to the *belláneh*. A little platform was pulled into the centre of the court. In about twenty minutes, the drums registered the bride's approach with a rapid zanging. Come forth! Come forth! commanded the wild drums. Come forth! Come forth! thrilled the *zaghareet*. Come like the full moon in thy ancient splendour! Shine to the glory of Islam! The door opened and, inch by inch, Hahja Bala led over the threshold the shapeless golden bundle. Peaked headdress, epauletted jacket, flaring tunic, bulging trousers—all were solid gold. The pair of false braids hanging over her shoulders to her knees scarcely stirred, so slowly did she advance. A square of red silk, which fell from the front of her headdress, completely covered her face. Fire-pots were held before and above her and in a maze of bridal incense—aloes-wood, musk, and amber—and delirious joy-cries she was huddled up to the platform where, about to be exhibited for the approval of the assembly, she assumed the traditional, stiffly coy posture, her sanguine fingers outspread at her waist. 'All that love Allah, give praises to Him now!' shrieked Hahja Bala fiddling with the pins that held the red curtain in place. 'Praise the glorious Prophet! All homage to Mohammed!' The drums, the frantic trilling, urged her to hasten, but the *belláneh* must not hurry. Mindful of the Evil Eye, she must not appear to flaunt the bridal face. With reluctance and holy shouts, rather, she strives to avert the awful consequences of envious admiration.

The curtain fell away finally. Ah, then what shouts went up! 'Blessings!' 'Blessings!' 'Praise the glorious Prophet!' 'May thy husband approve thee!' 'All homage to Mohammed!' 'O bless ye the Prophet!' 'Blest be this night, O Kadusha!' 'Blest be the Night of the Entrance!'

THE NIGHT OF THE
ENTRANCE

Early that evening, shortly after the sunset Call, the bride was taken in a closed carriage to her future home where the women and children of Kalipha's family received her. Persian rugs and rich hangings, borrowed from merchant friends, had transformed his crude little room into a nuptial chamber. Here, seated cross-legged upon the bed, in her stiff vestments, with covered face, hands motionless in her lap, Kadusha awaited the coming of her husband.

Out in the court great glass lanterns, suspended from the walls and cross-beams, shed festive brightness upon the revellers, upon the Seat of the Bridegroom, the pale blue throne that stood ready to receive him. 'Tread, tread, O my joy!' wailed the minstrels, 'Unite me to my beloved. By Allah we will intoxicate ourselves. Under the jasmine tree we will acquaint ourselves with rapture, and none shall reproach us. Tread, tread, O my joy! Allah hath ordained our sweet madness!'

The marriage procession, in the meantime, was forming around the corner. The cataclysmic noise of it starting on its way was my signal; in the lane below Mohammed was waiting for me and together we skirted the crowds half running to get a front place on the kerb. We climbed upon an empty date-stall where we crouched on our knees in the darkness waiting for the tremendous tide of light and noise to break over us.

The *zaffeh* had set out from the mosque from the Hôtel de Sfax and was moving slowly forward, creeping at a turtle's pace with intermittent long pauses: by ancient Kairouan tradition, it must consume a full hour. We could not see it yet because of an abrupt turn in the road, but we could see the brilliant illumination upon the shopfronts, the massed onlookers. Now a sudden flare flooded them with wan rose or green, then a rocket fled up-up-up to spill its stars in the black sky. It was a lurid uproar—the powerful drums booming to different measures, the pipes squealing, an army of voices confusedly bawling scripture to popular song tunes and—swooping like gulls above the tumult—the hoarse shouts of the populace. Blest be the marriage of Courage! May Power go with thee! Blest be this night! Praise Mohammed the last of the Prophets!

'Ah c'est magnifique, ce bruit!' cried his namesake, squirming with impatience. Magnificent! It was mad, outrageous, the barbarous din of fanatics swarming to do holy war! Though I had heard it every Thursday night that I had been in Kairouan—it terrified me. A great fan of light preceded the *zaffeh* and presently it hove around the corner, slow-surging like a breaker. Antique lanterns towered on heads and shoulders, tall torches were carried staff-wise. First the singers of the Koran, several hundred strong, then the dervish Aissaouas massed around their sheik, after them, the burners of benjoin with uplifted fire-pots. At intervals, when the throng ceased to move—as if carried away by its vehemence—youths formed rings by locking arms and bowed from the waist in passionate unison. When the train swept onward, they bore one of their companions high on the palms of their hands.

At the end of the mob stalked Kalipha and his best men transfigured by footlights; on both sides and in front of them boys smaller than Mohammed carried long laths studded with candles. A fleecy burnous hung from Kalipha's head, the slit where the folds came together showed his whiskered, brown face, but, in the manner of the bridegrooms of Islam, he kept his stern eyes ahead, oblivious of the cries. 'Blest be thy marriage, ya Courage!' 'Blessed be this night!' 'Assistance from Allah and a speedy victory!' On either side of him, in silken robes, with flowers over their ears, paced his attendants—the corpulent Sallah with tall Shedlie on one hand; on the other Farrah, handsome, bronzed giant, ludicrously coupled with Babelhahj. Babelhahj in his biggest turban and loudest stripes trying his utmost to look austere! A few feet from our tipsy grand stand they paused in their wondrous dazzle. Voices shouted to us by way of letting Kalipha know just where we were, but the eyes in the black muzzle remained riveted on a point just above the heads of the crowd. 'You are lapping this up, don't deny it!' I thought of him as the light of his presence moved past us.

We slid to the ground and were carried along in the drove of woolly burnouses. It was past the hour as we tunnelled through The Way of the

Assassins and out upon Kalipha's broad lane. The front part of the procession, loudly singing, were already piling up the stairs and through the door of Number Twenty. No fear of surprising the women: they knew at what moment to vacate the court. The rest of us halted. Kalipha and his attendants seated themselves on a row of chairs mounted upon a daïs against the house-wall; the candle-bearers encased them with their lustres, from nails above their heads the men hung their lanterns. Only the groom's immediate party were left in the lane. A long wait ensued during which, within doors, the groups comprising the *zaffeh*, in exuberant succession, honoured him with séances. This is the moment when young, inexperienced bridegrooms are given last words of advice. Surely nobody could suppose that Kalipha needed any! Yet many leaned to address his ears in sober confidence.

It must have been another hour before the celebrations inside were over. As the last of the singing throng trooped down to the street, I slipped up the stairs. The womenfolk with lighted tapers were pouring back into the court. The black wraiths were brandishing their bare arms in a great shaking of tambours, clapping of cymbals, and high walloping of drums. There was a stampede about the door leading to the staircase, the excited women laughing, yodelling, their candles tilted at crazy angles. A little girl's hair caught on fire, but was slapped out before any harm was done. All at once Kalipha's draped head loomed above them, framed for an instant by the darkness from which he emerged. They threw themselves upon him in the most abandoned welcome. With shrill cries they shepherded him to the throne, where he seated himself, ignoring with superhuman composure their violent hugs and kisses, the hot tallow dripping upon his new fez and the burnous that Eltifa had had made for him. Poor Kalipha! The loreleis were rearranging the folds of his headdress, making trumpets of their hands to buzz in his ears, daring to toy with that moustache so handsomely waxed at the tips!

But now the drum beats—like pistol shots—proclaimed the coming forth of the bride. Hypnotized, they moved away from the throne and formed brilliant flanges of colour and candlelight on either side of the door. It opened, seemingly of itself, and Hahja Bala assisted her over the threshold. Blindfolded, her scarlet fingers posed stiffly at her waist, the rhombic gold shape was being slowly led towards The Seat of the Bridegroom, while the air shook with the magnificat of the women, the mad tumult of the drums. 'Salutations to the glorious Prophet!' Hahja Bala's cackling chant could sometimes be heard. Step by step by step, the feet of *larossa* groped forward in their high pattens inlaid with mother-of-pearl; once she stumbled slightly.

Kalipha's face was as it should be—absolutely expressionless—as he watched their faltering approach. When she was stood at last squarely in front of the throne in the full pour of the lanterns, the candles came clustering around her. Like little wings they fluttered just above the point of her headdress symbolizing those ideals to which the wives of The Faithful should aspire. But all the light seemed to emanate from *larossa* herself,—from the quivering gold of her raiment, the paste jewels of her diadem, sparkling blue, green, and purple, the red silk of her concealment. Only Kalipha was calm while this was being unpinned. And when, with a triumphant gesture, it was swept from the antic death-mask—The Bridal Face—his dark gaze was the same. Once, twice, three times she was pivoted for his inspection amidst joy-cries and galloping drums. 'Is she not beautiful?' 'Say. Is she not beautiful?' he was asked confidingly. But Kalipha arose, stepped down from his throne. Putting his hand through the sharp little angle of her arm he moved in full possession of his bride towards the nuptial chamber. The women followed, but only to close the door upon them.

Things quieted down after that. The musicians laid aside their drums, Kadusha's mother, Zorrah, and Hahja Bala made themselves comfortable on either side of the door. The guests disposed themselves for conversation and fished from their garments pumpkin seeds and pellets of loban; some occupied themselves with the making and serving of coffee. Little boys started to play roughly, the girls to amuse themselves with finger games. The subdued voices of the *zaffeh* came up from below; you could picture them in recumbent attitudes smoking and exchanging reminiscences in the rich shine of their lanterns.

'How long do you think it will be?' I asked Jannat over the rim of my cup.

'One does not know,' she shrugged. 'But soon, if it be the will of Allah. It takes a little while when the bride is young. And sometimes, if the groom is very tired or has imbibed a bit too freely—which is a sin—he goes off to sleep. In which case,' she finished blithely, 'it does not happen for oh—hours and hours!'

After about twenty minutes and two rounds of coffee, the minstrels dutifully gathered up their instruments and began to drone to the most lacklustre accompaniment. A little later the *belláneh* tapped tentatively upon the door, then curled up against the jamb again as one who hadn't expected a response. There was a general air of cheerful resignation to a wait that might stretch out until morning. When the door was tapped the next time Kalipha's voice could be heard; the door opened cautiously, and she passed in to him a bottle of olive oil. We took heart from this, began to stir about and to arrange ourselves nearer the door. Energy bounded back to the arms of the orchestra, gaiety and excitement rippled once more. The men had started to sing.

Now we did not take our eyes off the door. But another quarter of an hour dragged by. Everybody except me still seemed very sure. I'll give him ten minutes more, I thought wearily. When I turned at length to go Kadeja stayed me with alarmed anxiety. 'You are not going? *B'Araby*, Sherifa, my uncle will never forgive you! Stay only—but see!' Her hand flew from my arm to her mouth in *zaghareet* for the door had been flung open long enough for Hahja Bala and Zorrah to rush in, and for an arm to toss something very red and white high over the bobbing heads into the centre of the court. There was a swoop for it, and the little shirt, stiff with newness, triumphantly bescarletted, was pawed over, and shrilly approved. It was the groom's virility that won their eagerest praise. 'Like a young lion, by Allah!' they screamed, hastily rubbing the chemise on their eyes before it was flung down the dark well of the staircase to be caught up and waved like a battle-flag above the joyous multitude. The house quaked—the lanterns were swinging—with the thunder of their thanksgiving. They were blessing the stains that proved the wife of Courage a virgin! Blessing—and twice blessing—the stains that proclaimed him so much a man!

THE LAST WINTER

In the spring before I went to France Kalipha and I had gone house-hunting, and had found, overlooking the wool-market, a charming little apartment, which, though tenanted at the time, was to be available for me upon my return. We had arranged it between us that during my absence I was to send him money enough to cover the rent for the first quarter, the cost of whitewashing and the purchase of the few necessary pieces of furniture. I was to leave the rest to Kalipha. 'You will have only to turn the key—and, *voilà*, you will be at home!' All summer I had luxuriated in that promise. It was something of a shock, therefore, to find on arrival that nothing had been done. Kalipha had a thousand elaborate excuses, but he depended upon me to understand the real reason, namely, that burying one wife and marrying another had taken every sou he could lay his hands on. Consequently, instead of a leisurely home-coming, work, expense, and despair rushed hand in hand to meet me.

But when I was finally installed those things fell away, leaving me with the blissful conviction that I was at home. How much the prospect from the window has to do with one's feeling for a place! The narrow road beneath me widened beyond to a diminutive common where the woolmarket convened on certain mornings each week. Road and common were faced with shops, in the doorways of which weavers sat at their looms talking and joking with one another.

The flat itself was light, compact, and small, though ample enough for Kiddypussy and me. The street door opened upon a flight of stone stairs leading up to a tiled entryway, at the far end of which was a commodious brick oven. There was but one room, red-tiled and lofty, with a window alcove that accommodated my work-table. In the left wall of this pleasant recess was a shelf-like cavity, obviously designed for storage purposes, but so deep and high that Mohammed appropriated it for his bed and decided, despite my protestations of fearlessness, that I could not be left alone at nights.

Everything pointed to a good winter. My first book had been accepted while I was away, and I was at work on another. There was money for everything—money put aside for my return to America in May; money, at last, to help Kalipha in another strenuous attempt to get back his permit before I left Kairouan. My efforts on behalf of his reinstatement as a guide had failed. The local officials would not lift a pen to help 'the brother of an assassin,' though every one of them grudgingly admitted that his record had been blameless. I had written letters to higher authorities in Tunis and in Paris, had even, it astonishes me to remember, addressed an appeal to the President of the French Republic himself! But I could find no one that would interest himself in the case. Now we were determined to try the Bey. Kalipha's nephew, Mohammed, who was caretaker of his Salambo estate, professed to be on warm terms with his employer, and he had promised us that, at his first opportunity, he would intercede for his uncle. I was dubious as to what the Bey could do, even if he would—so little power remains him. Nevertheless, I tried to manufacture faith of scepticism since my friend was absolutely certain that Mohammed's genius would work the miracle. During the winter Kalipha went twice to Tunis, each time in the hope of an audience with His Excellency. But nothing ever came of these negotiations, and to date, so far as I know, Kalipha has not regained his old title, *Le Guide Courage*.

As for Kalipha's domestic affairs, they had greatly improved with his marriage to Kadusha. His insistence that she could weave was not— what I feared—just a desperate attempt to justify his choice of a virgin. For her name *was* known among the rug merchants as one of their most qualified artisans. Moreover, she was fun-loving and affectionate, eager to be on good terms with all the family, and particularly Kalipha, of whom, wonderfully enough, she seemed genuinely enamoured. Kalipha, however, found much in her that called for correction: she was 'giddy,' she was 'headstrong,' she was 'sometimes sullen,' but, on the whole, he was not displeased with Kadusha, especially when he learned from the women that she was pregnant. *She* never mentioned her condition to him, even after it had become apparent. When I asked Kalipha if this was not unusual, 'Oh no,' he said. 'A wife has shame to speak of such things to her husband!'

In November, the joint household was called upon to find room for another family. Ever since the death of Zinibe, her husband's fortunes had steadily declined. Sallah, in his discouragement, had taken to gambling, as a result of which his shop was closed most of the time. Sallah's poor sister Ummulkeer was at her loom night and day to keep his children and his aged mother from starving. For two years the men of the family had done what they could to redeem Sallah. After they had given him up in disgust, it was Eltifa who kept him out of jail by secretly pawning her gold bracelets. The next thing we heard was that Sallah had absconded. Then, without hesitation or question as to how it could be done, Abdallah and Kalipha gathered into their home Ummulkeer, and old Ummi Sallah, Mohammed, Awisha, Hedi, Bashir, and little Sadoc.

It was wonderful to see that small house expand and adapt itself to seven additional persons, five of whom were children! Eltifa and Abdallah willingly bore most of the strain. Poor patient Abdallah could scarcely find the space to spread his prayer-rug, and they shared their bed with as many as could squeeze under the covers. Discomfort there was of necessity for everybody, yet with what good nature and patience all accepted the situation, what harmony was achieved, and what fun!

From the diary I kept that last winter I have culled, almost at random, a few of those little scenes and happenings that made it, of the three winters lived in Kairouan, the most precious.

December 7th

Dinner is over. Out in the court Ummulkeer and Kadusha sit side by side at their loom in a wheel of lamplight. Eltifa is furnishing the yarn for the rug they are making; when it is sold all three will share the proceeds. There is the pleasant jing-a-jing of the *kulehlas*.* The two Mohammeds are carrying up water, stopping on the stairs for a fist-fight. Everybody flies to separate them, and the combatants emerge with angry shouts and tears. But Kalipha and I refused to be exercised. The room is warm, we have eaten well, we recline smoking and quietly talking over the small happenings of the day. Baby Sadoc, the tiger-faced, wanders in. He

* the *kulehla* is an iron comb for pushing down stitches. To it are attached metal amulets of fish and Hands of Fatma, which serve a double purpose: protecting the work against the Evil Eye and providing a brisk little tune without which they say weaving becomes tedious

sits himself beside the fire-pot, keeping his eyes upon Kalipha until he has ascertained his mood. Boyh Abdallah parts the curtains, stoops, and comes in to sit in his usual place against the wall. He has on his new burnous—a vast tent of rough wool—so much the brown of his face that, were it not for those shining eyes, one might be put to deciding where one leaves off and the other begins! Little Awisha follows with the tea-tray, which she places before him, then disappears for his brazier. She returns holding it high on one hand. The blue tea-pot is already simmering upon it. Eltifa comes next; she lowers herself ponderously beside us on the bed. Again I remark to her brother how the room invariably brightens with her entrance. She chuckles when he tells her this and pronounces her one French word, 'Merci!' The children swarm about her and she loves it, Hedi and Bashir, cute youngsters of maybe five or six, find shelter beneath Abdallah's cloak. Eltifa begins winding the black yarn into balls. The tea is ready and Awisha takes a grave delight in passing out the cups. 'To thy refreshment' we bid one another. Eltifa and Abdallah are handed their evening cigarettes. They have no appetites to give them—they are simply a part of the little ritual. The girls are making so merry outside that Eltifa pretends to rail them for their lack of progress.

'Ya Ummulkeer! Ya Kadusha!' she calls mockingly. 'Is it that you have been pensioned by the Bey you can spend a lifetime on my carpet?' Their saucy answer, which they would not have dared to make had she been really serious, makes everybody laugh. A tantalizing odour begins to steal into the room, and presently Awisha serves each of us a handful of toasted grain, a little salted. During the course of the evening Kalipha decides to put Hedi and Bashir through their paces, Koranically speaking. His idea of fun is often abysmally benighted. Protesting, apprehensive, first one, then the other, must sit before him and bawl out those precepts with which Kalipha himself seems none too familiar since an amused Abdallah must occasionally prompt him. The little boys are soon in tears—for their blunders have apparently been enormous. Yet the pedagogue persists in cuffing and correcting them until he chances to ask for the parting song. Then—what relief—the pair, tear-stained and incoherent, awake a storm of claps for exactitude and vim! Over the next round of tea Abdallah tells us the story of Bueddam, The Father of the World, who lived alone on this earth for forty years 'with nothing to eat or to wear.' Midnight comes too soon. Mohammed and I must wrench ourselves from the cheerful warmth. The streets are deserted under a cold starlight. When we enter the stairway, Mohammed recites the litany against djinns until I get the lamp lit.

December 10th

No bedouin need starve nowadays. He has only to stuff a sack full of lush green grass, shoulder and trot it to Kairouan. There is five francs, anyway, in it for him. A good harvest is predicted; weeds grow luxuriant on the house-tops. What the country must be! One day soon, Kalipha says, we will hire donkeys and make our long-promised visit to Elmetboostah.

The *muezzins* had called, the after-sunset sky was rolling in rose. The air was still soft from the heat of the day as we walked out beyond the ramparts and along the road towards the ancient aqueduct, the favourite stroll of promenaders.

Kalipha was wearing my black sports-coat in which he cuts an absurd figure. It is a perfectly disreputable-looking old thing, and I passed it on to him thinking only that it would reinforce his burnous. But he thinks so highly of it that he wears it, as he says, *simple*. It's much too small for him and buttoned into it he looks about to pop. Then, as it is modishly short, beneath the waving hem, there is a consternating display of skinny, bare, brown legs, lavender garters, green socks and huge, mustard-coloured shoes! 'But it doesn't become you!' I tell him. 'What is that to me?' he says jauntily. 'I like it.' So he struts along, his hands stuffed deep in the sagging pockets. He assures me that no one suspects it of being a lady's coat. Sometimes he tells them it belonged 'to my brother,' sometimes, 'to my fiancé.'

Well, to go on. When we had walked a little beyond the hospital, we turned around. Kairouan was by this time atwinkle. Kalipha abruptly excused himself 'to consult' the fence. I sauntered on, hoping he would catch up with me before two magnificent promenaders at some distance behind me had passed. He was unconscionably long. I turned, half expecting to see him hiking haltingly up, instead, he was at his wall and, having consulted it, was standing there engrossed in admiration of the last light—a mere quill of primrose laid upon the horizon. He summoned me to join him just as the white-turbaned ones were within a yard of me. How willingly I could have wrung the neck of my guide, philosopher and

THE LAST WINTER

friend! How earnestly, after innumerable humiliations of this sort, how firmly and how, as I supposed, finally, have I told him that he must—simply must—wait till the coast is clear! The gentlemen swept by, courteously bidding me the salutations of the evening. As it was evident that I did not mean to join him, Kalipha came along, singing under his breath. I lit into him angrily. He stopped in surprise, regarding me—the brown old monkey—with his head cocked, eyes roguish, hands deep, chest robin-plump, spindly shanks ending in those outrageous clod-hoppers! And for the life of me, I couldn't keep from laughter. There was nothing to do but remind myself that he is worth ten such polished sons of the Faithful—and hope for better luck next time.

At the coffee-house outside the city walls, we watched the night settle broodingly. Bedouins were shooing their animals into the *fondook*—husky voices, throaty gurgles, sibilant *zahhhs*, patient moos, a bedlam of baas. Then sudden silence, that wide silence, the far sad silence of the plain. White stars glimmered, there were footfalls somewhere off in the dark, from the road a voice, poignantly clear, and the tidy clip-clip of a donkey tripping homeward.

December 15th

Yesterday was miserably cold, drizzling off and on until evening. At noon Kalipha brought in a fire-pot filled with new fire. I noticed that the edges of some of the coals were still black, but I was too grateful for the warmth to be concerned. He was to escort an English woman to the performance of the Aissaouas a little later, so he ordered a coffee from the window and sat himself down for a cigarette. I went on reading. After a time I realized that, although I was turning the pages, I was following only strings of words. My head had begun to ache. I had a curious sensation of having left the body that was sitting at my table. Baba Kalenie had come in with Kalipha's coffee and they were talking; their voices sounded miles below me. I was swimming high in far-off space. It was exhilarating, at the same time my head was thumping, my heart bounding with wild joy. Strange emotions lifted me to religious ecstasy at one moment, dropping me the next to hopeless despondency. Like the drowning, I reviewed my life, and my horror at its selfishness, its insincerity, melted into intense longing to make something finer of it. I would try harder, from that very moment regeneration was to be my grail.

141

I was burning up with fervour, tears scalded my eyes. Yet, immediately after, the profound futility of striving, of living at all, overpowered me, and I dropped my head between my arms.

'What is it?' Kalipha asked very gently.

'I think it is the fire,' I murmured, getting up and opening the window. I turned and, as I stepped back into the room, I fell into his arms. I had never fainted before. The-next-thing-I knew, as they say in books, I was on the floor, and Kalipha was calling my name and doing things to my face with a wet cloth. I began to vomit, reassuring him between retches. In another three minutes, I was asking for the details as I brushed my teeth.

But the incident did not end there. For Kalipha's own head had started to ache, and he had gone so pale that I urged him to go home to bed, insisting I felt well enough to accompany his tourist. He must have been pretty sick, because he consented.

In truth, there was nothing I felt less equal to that afternoon than the Aissaouas. After two hours of their mad drums, my head was blinding me with its pain. It was dinner-time before the séance was over, but I went directly home, too ill to care whether Kalipha was dead or alive.

I was asleep, lying across my bed in the darkness, when Mohammed came in tears to tell me that, although his father was 'very, very sick,' if I needed someone, Eltifa would come. I was feeling a lot better—I found when I got to my feet—so I went back with him.

My poor friend! He was as yellow as saffron under a great mound of covers, his head wrapped in a turban-like bandage, also yellow. His voice was feeble, full of sighs and groans—and curses for Kadusha whenever she changed the applications. The whole family was gathered dismally around, Mohammed crying silently. Abdallah had burned one of the preservative chapters of the Koran—to no purpose, I saw by the frightened faces. The life of the house was stopped, as if the last sacrament had been administered, and we were waiting for the death-rattle.

Presently Kalipha went off to sleep. All of us—even the littlest— kept very still, hardly daring to whisper for fear of disturbing him. When he awoke we knew, without his telling us, that he was better. Nevertheless, Ummi Sallah took as much salt as she could hold in each hand and, while her fists travelled slowly over his entire body, she was murmuring the prayers for driving out djinns. Pretty soon, one after another of us started to yawn: the remedy was taking effect.

Kalipha felt, oh, ever so much better when Ummi Sallah had done! He sat up and even consented to take that hideous thing off his head. Ummi Sallah—bless her—went away motioning to me with cast-up eyes that there was nothing to beat this panacea.

Today Mohammed confided in me that last evening, before he came to fetch me, his father was convinced that he was dying. So, like a true Mohammedan, he summoned Eltifa and Abdallah that he might arrange his worldly affairs. He told them the exact sums that were owing him by the merchants; of his own small debts. If he was spared, he would praise Allah as never before. But if he was, as he suspected, 'for the other world,' he was never one to question the divine decree. He advised them to get an advance from his debtors to give him a good funeral; what money remained they were to keep. Mohammed and Kadusha, and his child in her womb, he bequeathed to them! But what worried him was Sherifa. Who was there to look out for her when he was gone? Abdallah and Eltifa were both weeping as they pledged with the most solemn oaths to be my guardians.

Mohammed told all this merrily, as something to amuse me. He was dumbfounded when he discovered that I was crying.

December 28th

For almost a week now Ummulkeer has had bad eyes. When I first noticed them, I got some boracic powder in the French town and showed her what to do. Kalipha put some of the solution in a bottle which he gave her with instructions to bathe them several times a day. Last night her eyes were worse—so swollen she could hardly see. They wouldn't be any better, she told me despondently, until she had attended a *fokkarah*; she had the same trouble last year and the drums had been the cure. It was no good asking whether she had been using the boric solution since everybody, including Kalipha, was agreed that it was no sickness *per se*, but a djinn holding out for a party.

Tonight, however, her eyes were so much better that I was plainly astonished. Ummulkeer laughed with delight and showed me the *hegab* sewed to her handkerchief. Abdallah had taken over the case.

She related how he had studied his holy books and was finally enabled to tell her the exact nature of the malady: during the night one of the children must have struck her without, of course, the word that is the

143

dread of djinns. An immediate 'Bishmella!' would have averted the evil. As it was, 'the djinn's power was in that blow,' or, as Kalipha elucidated, 'The eyes smelled the djinn.' This much, at any rate, I understand: Unimulkeer has a djinn in her eyes, or maybe one in each eye, and it, or they, will not be routed except by a *fokkarah*. Until it is convenient for the family to give her one, she must wear, as a sort of stopgap, the amulet Abdallah made for her. When I saw how her poor eyes had cleared, I could only agree that a *hegab*, at least faith in a *hegab*, is a better cure than boracic.

With Ummulkeer her gay self again, the whole household is wonderfully restored. While the women were busy with supper preparations, Ummi Sallah regaled the children with one of her quaint little stories—this time of a louse whose name was Din-Din ben Din-Din. Kadusha's spirits were soaring; she and Ummulkeer were finding no end of things to laugh about. 'Their heads are full of *fokkarah*,' said Kalipha with a grim smile, but he did not check them. When Abdallah came in from his rounds, he had peanuts for the children. Eltifa sputtered at his extravagance, but even little Sadoc knew that she was teasing.

THE LAST WINTER
(CONTINUED)

A visit from Sidi Mohammed of Salambo is always a tremendous event in the family. He arrived unexpectedly yesterday afternoon and left this morning for a few days with Kadeja in Elmetboostah.

We dined very sumptuously last night—nothing is too good for Mohammed. There was soup to begin with, then *cous-cous*, such as only Kalipha can make, a magnificent dish of burrol besides, as well as a little leg of lamb, prettily spiced, and wearing a pantalette of frilled paper. For dessert there were oranges, dates, and roasted chestnuts. Everything had been ordered for Mohammed's comfort. The women, excepting Eltifa, and the children did not come into the room all evening. Yet for all the awe with which he is regarded, for all his fine clothes, his smooth turban and cultivated speech, Mohammed is as unaffected as Kalipha or Abdallah.

The evening was devoted to discussion of many things, the principal subject being religion, which was inevitable since Mohammed and Abdallah are both, each in his own way, authorities in El-Islam. Most of the time Mohammed talked and the others listened as respectfully as if he had been the *Bash Mufti* sermonizing from the Friday pulpit in the Mosque of Sidi Okba. He spoke and gestured with scholarly precision and, although I couldn't understand much of what he was saying, I felt that I could listen all night to the beautiful cadences of his voice. He questioned me concerning the religions of America; unfortunately there was not much I could tell him that he did not already know. This was a rare opportunity, I thought, to clear up some of my perplexities about djinns. Instead of answering my questions, however, Mohammed put others to me. Where do these demoniacal beings live? Of what are they made? What is their nature? Who is their chief? How do they appear? Wishing to do credit to my teachers, especially Abdallah, I explained as carefully as I could, my understanding of djinns, efreets, and sheytans. 'Have you ever *seen* one of them?' Mohammed inquired with his kindly smile. 'Has anybody that you know actually—and with his own eyes—seen a djinn?' I realized then that, far from being pleased at my precocity, Mohammed was deeply disturbed. Leaning forward in his earnestness, he assured me that there were thousands of modern-thinking Arabs like himself, who found it impossible to believe in the djinns and 'such superstitions.' As Mohammed does not speak French, Kalipha had to translate, passage by passage, all that was said in refutation of his firmest beliefs. I glanced apprehensively at Boyh Abdallah from time to time to see how he was taking such heresy. His eyes were twinkling with amusement, but he let his nephew talk on. A smile flickered across his gentle face when Mohammed explained that the only reason why Allah permits the practice of exorcism is because it furnishes many an innocent soul like Abdallah a means of livelihood! 'If you have power over djinns,' Mohammed turned to Abdallah, 'why do you not direct them to beneficial deeds? Why do you not command them to increase my fortunes and cure my accursed sciatica!'

His uncle laughed and from the paper cone in his hand poured a few toasted chick-peas into each cup. The reply that he made, when he had passed us our tea, was not really an answer. He never undertakes to treat a person, he said, until he has first ascertained whether his patient is 'sound in faith.' He professes no supernatural gift of healing: such power as he has is derived only from the word of Allah set forth in the blessed Koran and revealed by His prophet.

Sidi Mohammed said nothing to this, but during the course of the evening he told us several stories that substantiated his disbelief in djinns and djinn seizures. One particularly impressed me. There was once an Eastern prince. He had among his slaves a negress who took the opportunity, each time her master was absent, to have a djinn fit.

It was all that the terror-stricken women could do at such times to keep her from throwing herself into the well. Her tantrums were notorious before the Prince himself heard of them. But when he did, he gave orders that the next time she performed he was to be sent for. One day shortly after this, as soon as he had left the palace, the negress began to swoon and jabber and foam at the mouth. Accordingly the Prince was summoned. He came into the court at the climax, just as she was fighting her way toward the well. He looked on for a moment, then he fetched his walking stick and beat her until she shrieked for pardon.

Although Sidi Mohammed cautioned me against credulity in djinns, he impressed upon me the importance of the word *bishmella*. It is a positive force, he said, in warding off danger. It is on the lips of the Faithful at all times, in all places. Before eating one utters *Bishmella*, upon entering a dark room, before crossing the street, even before cuffing the cat. 'For it is,' he declared with eyes and finger upraised, 'the *principal* word!'

January 17th

Some of our nicest evenings this winter have been those spent with Kadusha's parents, Sidi Mohammed and Lella Zorrah. Last night Kalipha and I were there for dinner. It was an excellent meal—even Kalipha, who does not hesitate to say that he seldom eats food as good as his own, complimented Mohammed upon his wife's *cous-cous*.

Afterwards we drew close to the fire for the evening was cold. Their little son, Ali, an alluring baby, sat under his father's arm, gravely listening and watching. He is already jealous of his successor, still but a pod upon his mother's stomach. We were told of how he punches it scornfully, and when Zorrah complains of her burden he will say, 'My dear mother, my sweet, gentle mother, does thy stomach distress thee?' Zorrah smiled across at him. 'May Allah keep thee, for who have I but my son Ali?' He clambered earnestly to his feet, in answer to this, and planted kisses upon her face.

It was a delightful evening, as is always bound to be the case when Kalipha finds himself in congenial company. The conversation embraced aeroplanes, Kalipha's trip to Nefta when he was a guide, American skyscrapers, and the perils of infancy. Sickness, it appeared, is the very least of these. It was agreed that the thing most feared during the first six months of a child's life is the owl. For weeks after Ali was born their nights were full of terror. The wailing cries of the demon—the heart stops at the thought! It would knock against the shutters sometimes as it flew about trying to get in. Mohammed, seeing that I didn't understand, explained that the owl was once a woman, Lillith, the first wife of Adam. Some claim she was incarnated in this form, but it is generally believed that she strangled her child, and for punishment was turned into an owl. Be this as it may, the dreadful bird lives by infanticide. She fastens her talons into tender nurslings and sucks their blood.

Kalipha shook his head sententiously. 'It is no bird—this thing in feathers. Wood, mortar, bricks—nothing prevents her from smelling her prey. No good stuffing the key-hole and barring the shutters! Through a crack too small for a mouse or even an ant, she can get in if she wills! Ah, yes, my friend,' he nodded to Mohammed, 'I know what you suffered. When my son was born, didn't I sit up holding him tight in my arms night after night until dawn! While the spell was upon him the child was shrunken and yellow. But Allah preserved him, and the very instant the fiend lost interest and flew away, my son was entirely well!'

The fascinating subject was put an end to at this point by the entrance of a little boy who came to Sidi Mohammed several evenings a week for tutoring in the Koran. Our host excused himself and, in about half an hour, when the lesson was over, he resumed the conversation by telling us of a strange spell that is being exerted upon his pupil's family by the house in which they live. Ever since they moved in, six months ago, they have had nothing but trouble. First the boy fell ill of a mysterious malady; now the mother is languishing and unless they quit the house at once it is to be feared that she will die. The dwelling has an aura, heavy, like that of a tomb. Kalipha asked its location; my thoughts, like his, were back in the house we had lived in last spring and for a moment I felt the clammy dread that had hung over us there. 'Do you hear, Sherifa!' exclaimed Kalipha. 'I am not surprised! It is the same! Let us thank Allah, the Merciful, the Compassionate, that we are out of that place!'

When we had done marvelling over the coincidence and our deliverance, I asked the men what caused such a malevolent atmosphere. In Mohammed's opinion, murder was committed there; djinns linger about the scene of a crime. Or, Kalipha suggested, it might be an *efreet*, the ghost of a dead person. He said that in former times a saint was often interred beneath the pavement of his own court. Then he told us this curious story.

A number of years ago, Sallah Kablutie unknowingly moved his family into such a house. One night when Ummulkeer and Zinibe were seated at their loom, someone passed behind them. It was a distinguished old man with a long white beard and eyes—proud and fierce—beyond all imagining. Ummi Sallah saw him, too. After that the apparition appeared—but only to Ummulkeer—again and again. Once it spoke to her. 'You must leave this house. You must leave this house.' It was repeating the words as it faded and mingled with the air. Naturally the women were terrified. Wherever they went they talked of their experience and some strange facts were thereby revealed. They were told that the house stood vacant most of the time; tenants moved in—and moved out telling the same story. Those were wise that left as soon as they were warned; for disasters rained down upon them that didn't.

The women carried these tales back to Sallah and begged him to move, but he dismissed them as idle talk. 'Mister Sallah,' said Kalipha with a scornful toss of the head, 'was above believing myths. Well, my friends, his trade fell off. His children died at birth—one, then another, and still another. After the death of the third—his first son, at that—Sallah was frightened and they moved. But the spell was upon them. Calamity followed calamity—sickness, business reverses, accidents, and finally the death of Zinibe. That was the worst, but it was not the last. Now the barber-shop is closed, Ali, the oldest son, has gone to the devil, Sallah has followed him, and his little ones are orphaned. The curse of a house, my friends—I tell you there is nothing worse!'

I suggested that maybe it has worked itself out by now; maybe, when the worst that can happen has happened, the curse dissolves? Kalipha looked dubious, 'Who knows? All we can say is, *Mektoub*.'

January 22nd

Kalipha left this morning for Tunis to be gone at least a week, and Mohammed has assumed his place at the head of the household. Tonight the two of us ate in lonely state, Kadusha submitting to his commands with little grace—for which I could not blame her. While we were having our coffee, a wedding procession passed the house and the girls rushed to peep through the shutters. I thought Mohammed had suddenly gone crazy, he was waving his arms and shouting at them, ordering them with dire threats away from the window. Not knowing what it was all about, I begged him to calm himself. 'It is not possible!' he cried angrily. 'You know nothing of these women! Once before when my father was absent I permitted her a look. You should have seen her! It was as if she would eat the honey and lick the pot as well!' He made an airy scoop with his fingers and stuck one in his mouth, by way of illustration.

149

'But surely one little peep—'

'Oh, no, Sherifa! Oh, no, oh, no!' he shook his head emphatically. 'One cannot permit such things. You do not know the Arab woman.'

'Mohammed is right,' said Abdallah. So laughing, but regretful, the girls sobered down to their tasks and pretty soon Ummulkeer was telling a story of a sultan's son—always a sultan's son.

January 24th

Authority has made Mohammed insufferable. He has a new voice, very loud and shrill, and when Kadusha fails to please him, or, succeeds in displeasing him, as he would have it—he puts on Kalipha's famous manner with remarkable accuracy: the leer, the head-wagging, the oily insinuation and mockery. Dinner was a stormy scene over the fish soup she had made. When the others came in for the evening he was still reviling her for having left in the bones. Eltifa said something to him in mild reprimand that caused him to rear like a charging bull, and when Abdallah, too, expressed displeasure, Mohammed got into his shoes and dashed out of the house. However, we managed to get through the evening without him. Eltifa spun the soft brown wool, Abdallah made tea, the girls were very gay and the children played Dome of the Sultan and Where goes the Caravan? Later, Ummulkeer and Kadusha left their work to entertain us with a play. Ummulkeer was the Wife of the Bey's Son; she was supposed to be a little Fey. Over her high headdress (a bunch of wool) she wore a silk shawl (Kadusha's hip-scarf) and her stomach was distended with royal fruit (also wool). She comes in, simpering and chittering, to pay a visit on her friend. After the usual formalities have been parried back and forth, Kadusha gives the half-wit a pail to sit on. The audience yell with glee. The Wife of the Bey's Son is scandalized and threatens to report the breach of respect. Nevertheless, the conversation shuttles very merrily between them. Friend Kadusha is treated to all the gossip of the Bey's household—what his wife has to put up with, what they have for their meals, to all of which she listens with the most ardent attention, plying for more. When her fine guest gets up at last to go, the royal progeny falls—to the mild horror of both. Kadusha picks it up and hands it to the Wife of the Bey's Son who hurries off crying that she must take the tidings to the Bey!

February 9th

The first night of another Ramadan. After supper Kalipha and the two Mohammeds attended the service at the Great Mosque, Abdallah was out with his tea. If his small blue pot were as big as a cauldron it could not quench the Ramadan thirst of his clients. We stay-at-homes felt something of the cordial spirit abroad in the world of men. Even though we sat in our accustomed places, doing the same things we had done all winter, there was a pleasant difference. The night was subtly marked for enjoyment: unexpected nice things could happen, but even if they didn't, the evening would not be stereotype or humdrum. In mellow mood, we waited confidently for the curtain to go up.

When I handed Eltifa her cigarette, Ummulkeer roguishly held out her hand for one too. Her devilishness was hailed with shocked laughter. The curtain had lifted. We were too keen for the show to offer more than the faintest discouragement. The children jumped and squiggled with excitement. When we had all promised that we wouldn't breathe a word of her caprice to the men, Ummulkeer put the cigarette to her lips and took a deep-chested pull. Her prankish sparkle changed to a startled look and at about the fourth pull her eyes went vague, visionary. She sank back against the wall and began to mutter and moan, tossing dreamily from side to side as if to the tom-toms. 'Sidi Heshmi! It is Sidi Heshmi!' screamed the children beginning to caper. Laughing, almost as excited as the children, Eltifa and Kadusha hitched close to Ummulkeer in an effort to make out what she was saying. 'Her djinn husband, Sidi Heshmi!' Kadusha explained to me with a wise smile. 'The smoke is arousing him!' It was the first I knew that Ummulkeer had a djinn husband. To my astonishment I learned that she had had him for years! Sidi Heshmi was being greeted by all with an elaborate deference, but with a happy warmth, too, that proved him a confirmed favourite. 'Tell him welcome, Sherifa!' Eltifa cooed, 'Say "Welcome in the great name of Ullah!"' which I did.

His weird gibberish, bubbling from the mouth of Ummulkeer, puzzled them excessively. Only now and then a word or a phrase was distinguishable, as for instance when she had smoked the cigarette to within half an inch of the tip we caught the word 'cigaro.' She was relieved of the hot butt, yet the 'cigaros' persisted with plaintive frequency till I lit her another. When Kadusha tried playfully to take the cigarette out of her hand Ummulkeer cowered, whimpering like an injured idiot.

Sidi Heshmi was asked all manner of questions: Where is Sallah Kablutie? When will he return? Will their carpet sell? His enigmatic replies made no more sense than the lingo from which they were disentangled. It needed Abdallah to interpret such cryptic utterances as 'The water was up to his waist,' 'Hot,' 'Seven,' 'Under the millstone, Y'Sidi!' With everything Eltifa and Kadusha could think of they endeavoured to placate him and bribe him back to slumber. But Heshmi would have none of their pomat, their orange-blossom water and benjoin. It was clear to me, at least, that he was getting what he wanted; Ummulkeer, smoking for the first time in her life, was having a glorious time!

The youngsters were taking full advantage of her trance, romping and yelling as they never do when she is in command. Yet, despite their wild antics Ummulkeer was almost successful in retaining that faraway look. It was funny, though, when Hedi knocked over the lamp to see her make a wild grab for it! I thought the game was up. A suspicion—just the shadow of a suspicion—that she was shamming entered the minds of the women. They merrily reproached her and teased her to admit that she was only fooling. Poor Ummulkeer, looking terribly embarrassed, sank back and took refuge in her unearthly mutterings. It worked, too. Every vestige of doubt instantly vanished!

She was on her third cigarette when Abdallah darted into the house on an errand and was called upon to appease the visitor. As busy as he was tonight, he came in, looking very much amused. Crouching before Ummulkeer he welcomed Sidi Heshmi with that beguiling politeness usually reserved for the very old and small children. After a few courteous inquiries, and just before he seized his tea-pot and popped out of the door, he gave Ummulkeer a sound swat on her behind!

She revived with remarkable suddenness. We were all laughing but not, it appeared, over the same thing. The others were laughing with joy that Ummulkeer was restored to them. As for answering their eager questions she hadn't the slightest idea what they were talking about, simply had no recollection of anything that had happened after she had put the cigarette to her mouth. Her face was blank innocence while they enlightened her. 'Did I say that!' she marvelled. 'Then what did I do?'

She was as bashfully delighted by our teasing as a girl who has entertained her first beau. Curious as to what she would say, I slyly suggested that if smoking did that to her...

'But it was not the cigarettes!' she hastened to assure me. 'By the Prophet, Sherifa! By thy dear head, I swear it was not the cigarettes!'

'Oh, no!' Kadusha flew to her support. 'Not the cigarettes! It was because she did not dance on the night of the *fokkarah*.'

'But Ummulkeer did dance!' I exclaimed. 'She was dancing with you out there in the court.'

'Ah *that!*' the girls smiled, shaking their heads. That wasn't the same; she should have danced right up close to the drums. They did not explain why she hadn't.

GUEST OF THE BEDOUINS

I t was barely seven o'clock, but our donkeys could scarcely make their way along the streets and through the teeming bazaars. From fry-shops, coffee-houses, and food-stalls voices hailed us above the din. 'May thy morning be light unto thee!'

'May thy morning be blessed!' 'May the peace of Allah go with thee!' The whole town seemed to know that Kalipha, Mohammed and I were bound for Elmetboostah.

Word had reached us that Sidi Farrah had recently been appointed sheik of his *douar*. As soon as he heard the news, Kalipha rushed off to hire donkeys: we must go at once, the very next day, to felicitate our friend on his appointment.

We wove our way across the roaring market-place, devoted at this hour to the traffic in camels, then an arched gate through the ramparts let us out at last upon the plain. The impact of the silence was deafening. The air was soft, vaporous, marvellously transparent; the low blue hills to the left had stepped boldly forward and figures at some distance on the road stood out with the precision of objects seen through a stereoscope. On either side of the road the scattered cemeteries lay as calm as snow upon the slopes of their mosques, here and there a veiled figure moved among the little domes. Now, from afar off, we could hear the wailing chant of mourners—of bedouins that during the night had brought their dead for burial in the consecrated earth of Sidi Abdelli. Kalipha caught the burden of their dirge and began to drone, '*Yowleedy, yowleedy!* My son, O my son! Proud wert thou as the son of many sultans, thy approach was like a banner, thine was the strength of a camel, where is he that could equal thy prowess? Who will bring in the beasts now, *yowleedy*? Who will give them to drink?' The threnody trailed off into a long, heartbroken wail.

'There is no strength or power but in Allah,' murmured Kalipha. Then quite cheerfully he said, 'Ah yes, my friend, to Allah we belong and to Him we must return!' The thought of being dead on such a morning might have sobered us had the sun been less warm, the sky less blue. The almond trees in the garden of Drat Tomar were blossoming, azure wind-flowers made mosaic of the grass and from the sky a lark spiralled its pure song. Mohammed, always in the lead, began to sing at the top of his voice. Much persuasion had been necessary to induce Sidi Hassein to release his young apprentice for our expedition. The swing of the tassel on Mohammed's fez, the lively jig of his heels against his donkey's sides proclaimed his jubilance.

The gardens behind us, we were crossing the plain in good earnest. The air smelled succulent and green like the rind of water-melon, the bland April sun smiled upon the broad earth—it was good to be alive and bound for Elmetboostah! At long intervals a 'caravan' of itinerant farmers passed. The camels in the lead bore the menfolk, then the donkeys, festooned with mill-stones, chickens, looms, antediluvian plough, sickles, and earthenware. The women, their babes secured to their hips or backs, trudged in the rear belabouring the donkeys. There was always the same hearty exchange of greeting, 'May thy path be broad!' 'And thine twice as broad!' Sometimes a dark mound between us and the horizon bespoke a bedouin encampment, then, for stretches, it would seem as if we were the only living creatures upon the *bled*.

Mohammed continued to trip ahead at the same jaunty pace, but Kalipha and I, quite early in the journey, had discovered that we were mounted less fortunately. By eleven o'clock Kalipha was having to whack and villify his Gris-Gris to keep him even in motion, while no curse was horrible enough, no switch sufficiently sharp to induce my Modestine to exceed the gait of a snail. I was starved, my thighs ached, and a loathing of donkeys consumed me. Kalipha's swarthy face had gone black, his voice from strenuous usage had become a kind of croak. We were toiling along like mutes on the way to a funeral, when suddenly Kalipha brandished his walking-stick and began to bawl, 'Turn to the right! To the right!' Far ahead Mohammed stopped, waited in doubt. I scanned the landscape for some particularity that might have served as guidepost. The road ran undeviatingly before us and, to the right and to the left of it, there was no path, no single track, not even a cactus clump to relieve the boundless monochrome. What monstrous caprice, then, was this? 'But Kalipha,' I wailed, for my spirit wilted at the prospect of travelling a single yard in the wrong direction. 'Shut up!' he barked. There was something Jovian about Kalipha's wrath. His curling black moustaches that at all times belied his good heart with an aspect of the most confirmed villainy, bristled dangerously.

In the meantime Mohammed, gesticulating, shouting, still blissfully unaware of the storm, invited the full force of it upon his head. Kalipha began to bellow like a demented bull. 'To the right! Thou idiot! Thou pig! To the right! And a curse upon her that bore thee!' It seemed as if his lungs must burst, but the mystified Mohammed did not budge. 'Thou dog! Thou base-born blockhead! A bane upon thy religion! May the dogs defile the grave of thy forefathers!' With each awful oath he spat his contempt. Even Mohammed's reluctant approach did not stem Kalipha's frenzy. He smote his brow, he seized his fez and flung it from him, he beat upon his breast, and in a voice that shook with fury invoked the eye of Allah upon a worthless son.

Mohammed joined us with uncompromising dignity. 'Make an end, Sidi, in all the sacred names of Allah!' he cried out at last and, after he had recovered his father's fez, we set off across the plain in the wake of Kalipha's intuition. Kalipha, ahead, still wrestled with his 'djinn,' behind me Mohammed showed every symptom of having been affronted beyond redress—of all mortals we were the most miserable and, that our mortification might be complete, the dry earth was wrinkled and cracked and the somnolent donkeys kept stumbling, to the peril of our necks. 'Take care!' Kalipha commanded over his shoulder, 'Look, do as I do!' We looked—in time to see a confounding tangle of hoofs and heels, a downfall of objects, as Kalipha and his Gris-Gris performed a complete somersault! Mohammed was on his feet before I had come to my senses. Breaking into loud wails, he ran toward the motionless heap. I hastened up—at the most maddening saunter—but Mohammed's tear-smudged face neither confirmed nor dispelled the dread that possessed me.

Like limb-locked lovers the fallen lay, the incorrigible Gris-Gris was sound asleep, while Kalipha, *sans* fez, slippers, walking-stick, and basket, was beet-red and helpless with what might be either mirth or convulsions. 'Look,' he choked, 'do as I do!' Our relief, thereupon, found vent in the most immoderate laughter, from which we rallied only to be seized with fresh paroxysms.

Things went better after that. Gris-Gris' downfall had a rousing effect upon the donkeys and laughter had limbered us. By way of peace offering, Kalipha explained, rather sheepishly, that it had been a sudden smell of the river that had determined our direction. But weariness, hunger, and the apparent aimlessness of the trek did not matter so long as we were friends!

The terrain rose and fell now in gentle undulations. Presently Kalipha drew up, and pointing with his stick, triumphantly announced, 'La voilà!' It was a moment before I could discern the douar—a dun-coloured mole upon the face of the dun-coloured earth. Scattered like haystacks the mud huts of Elmetboostah, with here and there a familiar black tent, climbed a slight slope. Half a mile to the west a thread of vivid green marked the course of the oued. For some time it was as if we approached a deserted village. We were within half a mile but, as yet, not a movement, not a sound, betrayed the little community. Then, quite suddenly, it sprang to life. Dogs began to bark; as if from ambush they rushed down upon us ready to tear us to pieces. Like a swarm of white ants came the men alternately cursing the dogs and hailing us, behind streamed the women, their blue draperies blowing, their silver bangles flashing as they shrilled the traditional reception of the women of Islam. Sidi Farrah, the sheikh, towered head and shoulders above the throng that soon surrounded us.

It was the first time I had seen Farrah ben Mustapha against his own background, among his own people. The white kafieh, or headcloth, gave the glow of bronze to his fine regular features. Over the eye, whose sight had been destroyed in the World War, he wore a black patch, but so far from disfiguring his handsome face it seemed rather a mark of distinction. There was a simple sincerity in Farrah's welcome as he helped us to dismount.

Kadeja's pleasure in our arrival made me ashamed that we had not come before. She embraced each of us in turn and, while she plied her uncle with questions, she embraced us all again praising the goodness of Allah. Suddenly conscious that someone had hold of my hand I discovered Boolowi. His chubby face beamed his civilities—he had not forgotten that we had been great friends in Kairouan. Mohammed had not forgotten either, for he seized my other hand with a menacing look for le petit sauvage as he always called Boolowi.

Kalipha walked away with the men and the women closed in around us. For generations they had tenanted and tilled this land, some of them had never been to town. I was a fabulous creature—a *Roumi!* With incredulous bub-bub-bubs and crows of rapturous delight they examined my rough garments, so graceless compared to their vivid head-dresses and classic draperies. If I had been told that these sinewy, bare-footed women were the last of the gods I think I would have believed it. Their eyes had the keenness of eyes accustomed to far distances, the sun had tanned their skins to the brown of a medallion, all had an antique regularity of feature, and young and old alike were slim and strong and straight. By comparison the Arab women of the city were cellar plants. Their eyes were dull, their complexions sallow, their features hybrid of innumerable races. It was doubtful whether all the hareems of Kairouan could produce one who, alongside these radiant plainswomen, would seem more than merely pretty.

Kadeja was pulling at my sleeve. 'Come, little sister, come refresh yourself!'

'Who is she?' they clamoured, ignoring Kadeja's impatience. 'Where does she come from?'

'From—Amelique,' said Kadeja, uncertainly.

'From Amelique?' they repeated, shaking their heads and looking to one another for enlightenment.

It was with difficulty that Kadeja extricated me. As we hastened toward the house one of the women caught up with us. 'For the love of Araby, Kadeja, where is this "Amelique"? Is it one of those *douars* in the neighbourhood of Sousse?'

Kadeja knew, at least, that America was not in the dominion of the Bey. 'It is far, far away,' she cried with a sweep of her arm. 'Farther even than Mecca. A great sea lies between Madamma and her country.'

The woman's jaw dropped. *'Wallah!'* she muttered. It was as if she realized for the first time that the Kingdom of the Bey did not constitute the whole world.

The home of the sheikh, like the other houses, was built of massive mud bricks and thatched with brush and straw. It was cool and dim and quiet within. A mud column divided the room into halves. One side served at once as kitchen, storeroom and larder. Here were sieves of shredded goat-skin, guns, and powder flasks, mill-stones, and camel-muzzles, donkey-paniers, and wooden bowls. Looms, spindles, carders, pestle and mortar and wet-weather clogs. Bright earthen drums for female amusement, folded tents and embroidered saddles. Brush-brooms of twigs and dried grasses, gaudy sacks hard with grain. Mats and ropes of esparto grass, fire-pots and fire-fans. Giant jars for oil and meal tipped against the wall, smaller jars for tomato paste and spices. There was even a sitting hen that clucked uneasily as I passed around the pillar to where the men were gathered. This half of the house consituted the living quarters. It was spread with vivid bedouin rugs, the whitewashed walls half-way up were covered with rush matting and the sole piece of furniture was the painted chest that contained the family wardrobe.

I took my place in the circle as Farrah and his kinsmen were solemnly pronouncing their satisfaction with our visit. We were all *deuf Allah*, guests of God, I gathered, dependent from day to day upon His bounty. While each one spoke the others interjected: 'By Allah, the great!' 'Yea, by Mohammed, the Prophet of Allah!'

Kalipha, who is, of course, absolutely unrivalled in verbal grace, heard them out with respectful attention. With finger upraised, then, he summoned the Prophet as his witness and pushing back his fez and taking a deep breath—as if he were about to launch upon one of his inimitable tales—he performed the *'necessaire'* on our behalf. With proverb and elaborate parable, interlarded with appropriate quotations from the Koran, he expressed our pride and pleasure to be the guests of Sidi Farrah. We were swooning with hunger, there were things we burned to discuss, but Arab etiquette is rigid and exacting.

Meanwhile in the doorway Kadeja fanned the fire under our meal. Beyond, at a distance that was barely discreet, an inquisitive assembly awaited our next appearance. Murmurs of approval greeted the last word of Kalipha's discourse and Kadeja bore in the *kassar*. It was heaped high with *cous-cous* garnished in our honour with chicken and raisins. We hitched nearer the bowl, the men as they rolled up their sleeves calling, perfunctorily: 'Come Kadeja, eat of Allah's bounty ' 'Eat with enjoyment! May it strengthen thee!' she responded from behind the pillar.

For the next few minutes no word was spoken except when Sidi Farrah, selecting some delicacy to lay at my place, exhorted me to eat. Kadeja replenished the bread flaps from time to time, her eyes discreetly downcast. Then, one after another, we dropped out, rendered Allah his

159

due, and, settling ourselves against the wall, paid our compliments to Kadeja's cooking with stentorian belches. Smiling this time, she reappeared with ewer, basin and towel for our ablutions. The fire-pot was placed before Sidi Farrah, and while he made the tea, Kalipha and Mohammed recounted the news of the town. Our hosts, in turn, had much to tell us about the winter rains. They had been so heavy this year that we had feared for the safety of our friends. Elmetboostah had been above reach of the flood, but in a nearby *douar* two women were drowned and there was scarcely a village that had not lost several dwellings.

Boolowi, who had not uttered a sound since our arrival, sat close beside me, his legs folded under him, hands clasped in his lap, perfectly content, apparently, to be seen and not heard—a model little mussulman. When he saw that I was watching him, he smiled timidly and with a furtive glance toward Mohammed whispered: 'Come, Sherifa, come with me!' Sidi Farrah was smiling. 'Boolowi wishes to conduct you through the *douar*,' he said.

We set out *en masse*, Mohammed, Boolowi and I heading a procession that rapidly recruited swarms of men and children. The *douar* was busy as a hive, and the workers were the women. Two of them were laying the foundation for a new dwelling, hoisting the blocks of mud into position one upon the other. On one side of the slope, six or seven half-grown girls were milking a double row of sheep, tied head to head. They hailed us with shouts and boisterous laughter and the men shouted back at them 'May Allah aid thee!' From the direction of the river straggled women bent almost double under the weight of their great water-jars; another group of animated maidens, each swinging a little hatchet, were off to gather firewood, while within the brush enclosure before each dwelling women were carding or spinning or weaving to the liveliest clatter of tongues. Some seated on the ground, their wooden bowls between their outstretched legs, worked oil and meal into granules for the supper couscous, others hovered like vestal virgins in the smoke of their cauldrons or, crouching, nursed the fires beneath their bread. At sight of us, work was abandoned. Their fingers flashed against their teeth as they let loose the welcoming *zaghareet*. Mohammed, Boolowi and I were drawn into the enclosures. 'In the name of Sidi Abd-ul-Kedar welcome, kin of Kadeja!' they clamoured. 'May Allah prosper thee!' 'May thy days be blessed with honey, milk and figs!' 'May Allah content and enrich thee!'

Kalipha had often described—extravagantly it had seemed to me—the lavishness of bedouin hospitality. I realized now that his accounts had been quite literal. Every house we stopped at offered us its best. The women plied us with pats of mutton butter wrapped in leaves, with handfuls of dates and loaves of bread, they overwhelmed us with bowls of camel-milk and stuffed our pockets with eggs. At one house they gave chase to a fowl and thrust it squawking dismally into my arms! Mohammed came to my rescue and for the rest of the promenade carried my disconsolate chicken by its legs.

In one doorway, a woman sat churning, singing as she did so to the surge of the milk. She smiled at us, but kept right on with her lusty work-song. The churn was the hide of a baby goat, four black knots were all that were left of its nimble legs, the withered neck served as both handle and spout, but bloated with milk the little hide looked ludicrously lifelike. The woman's song followed us as we sauntered on and the faces of my companions broke into broad smiles. 'Sister Shedlia honours thee in her song.' Kalipha explained. 'She is singing "Oh, Madamma is like a virgin bride. Her skin is fleece fresh from the washing. The sun is bright on her hair."'

The slope flattened toward the middle of the *douar*. Here, on a sort of common, were congregated all the men who had not joined the procession. They sat in scattered patches smoking and conversing.

'The men do not work?' I asked Kalipha.

He shrugged his shoulders. 'The seeds are sown, they await the harvest.' He studied me for a moment, then under his bushy brows his eyes began to twinkle. 'And for what reason does a man marry, *hein*?'

We were drawn into one of the circles and when, at length, we would have moved on, several of the men arose pressing us 'to honour their houses.' Of the calls we made that afternoon one, particularly, stands out in my memory. Sidi Hahj, our host, was reputed to be the wealthiest man in the *douar*, yet his house was neither larger nor in any wise finer than the rest. In the yard his wives and daughters-in-law were washing wool and laying the snowy strands to dry upon the hedge-brush, two of his sons were unearthing sacks of grain from a jar-shaped cistern. All tasks were laid aside, however, as Sidi Hahj ushered us into the house and the excited women whisked about preparing tea.

The talk in the circle reverted to a subject begun upon the knoll when it had been proposed that I choose a mate and settle down for life in Elmetboostah. 'By Allah!' cried Sidi Hahj, 'my last-born Mustapha seeks a third wife.' The innuendo provoked hearty laughter, the women drew the folds of their headdresses across their smiling faces, Sidi Mustapha was grinning.

'Though the countenance of your son pleases me,' I countered, 'I would, in truth, make a poor sort of bedouine for I can neither spin nor weave, neither can I plough nor thresh.'

'*Meselch!*' No matter! Sidi Hahj waved aside such demurs.

'Nor can I perform even those tasks that his wives would consider the simplest.'

'It is not for *labour* that my son would marry such a maiden!' exclaimed the poor boy's father. '*B'Araby*, he would wear thee as a Jewel in his turban!'

'But his other wives?' I suggested. 'They would hardly care for that.' This time it was Sidi Mustapha that spoke up. 'They are no problem. I would divorce them—phweet!' He blew them from the palm of his hand.

'Well said,' applauded his father above the laughter. The women were not making any attempt to conceal their merriment. 'Thou hast heard thy husband?' Sidi Hahj called to them. 'My daughters be warned '

'My master hath no need to divorce us,' one of them responded. 'If it be the will of Allah, we will remain to wait upon her.'

'*Kief-kief larossa!*' Like a bride of Araby! exclaimed the other, bearing in the tea-tray.

When we took leave of the amiable Hahj and his family the sun had dropped low and the village was noisy with returning flocks and herds. From the top of the knoll we watched the sun slip behind the horizon. Without an interval of twilight the cold dusk descended upon the plain and the moon grew faintly luminous as if to distract us from the lingering beauty of the west. The cold had driven most of the women indoors, the hill-top gradually cleared until only a few of us, muffled to the ears in our burnouses, sat on, so engrossed in talk that dusk deepened to dark unnoticed.

Sidi Farrah had asked me what I was taught to believe respecting the phenomenon of the sunset. Kalipha spared me the necessity of an unimaginative answer by explaining that I was both ignorant and misinformed. I believed, for instance, that the earth was round! Nevertheless, he had found me teachable, even eager to learn the knowledge that had been vouchsafed the children of Islam. His apology moved Farrah and his brothers to such concern for my intellectual darkness, that I was given, then and there, my first lesson in physical science.

The village had grown dark and quiet. Here and there a supper fire still burned and the women, as they glided to and fro, seemed more than ever like priestesses engaged in some mysterious rite, their voices subdued to a murmur. Above us stars shone from the unfathomable depths of the sky and all about the plain stretched as dim and vast and cold as infinity. Their version of the sunset seemed somehow remarkably plausible that night. At sundown every evening, I was instructed, a venerable dragon, known to the Arabs as 'Eight Pair of Horns,' waits just under the horizon. As the sun rolls off the rim—if the earth were round how could all this be?—Eight Pair of Horns catches it and, like a bird with a seed, flies, and flies—never stopping to rest his heavy wings—until he reaches the other edge of the world where he deposits the sun that it may rise again and shine to the glory of Allah.

As we walked back through the village my mentors promised to teach me many things during our stay among them. The dogs, ever alert for marauders, stopped barking at the sight of us and grudgingly permitted us to pass. Doorways gave us bright glimpses of supper circles. The chickens that had taken to their chilly roosts upon the housetops made comic silhouettes against the pale sky. One by one, as we passed their homes, the men dropped out.

Dinner was waiting when we arrived. I was chilled to the bone, but the room was warm and bright. Kadeja arose from beside the fire-pot to take our cloaks. We dropped to our places and in a moment the smoking bowl was set down in our midst. It held *lahsida*, a wheaten pudding crusted with sugar and swimming with oil. *'Ayia bishmella!'* the men called after Kadeja. Because we were *en famille* tonight I yielded to a wanton impulse—moving over I entreated Kadeja to join us. The little boys stared at me as if, although I persisted, they could not believe that I was serious. 'Come, eat of Allah's bounty!' I urged, patting the place beside me. Kadeja's eyes sparkled with amusement. 'Eat!' she responded, pantomiming the act. 'Eat with enjoyment!'

'But eat with us for my sake,' I insisted, 'for the sake of Sidi Abd-ul-Kedar, for the sake—'

Kalipha glared at me. 'Are you possessed?'

'Come join us, Kadeja,' said Farrah not unkindly. Kalipha was very annoyed with me, but he was obliged to add: 'Come along, Kadeja.'

She complied good-naturedly, however, she dipped but once in the bowl, then slipped away to prepare the coffees. Kalipha eyed me reproachfully. 'Thou knowest it is shameful for an Arab woman to eat in company with men!' On such points my friend was uncompromisingly orthodox.

With a smile of sympathy for my disappointment, Kadeja declared: 'Every morsel that you eat, little sister, rejoices my own stomach!'

While we sipped our coffees Kadeja ate her own supper screened from us by the pillar. A few minutes later, the evening tasks completed, she joined us. Boolowi left his place by the fire-pot to curl beside her on the painted chest. Farrah prepared a cup of coffee and passed it along to her. Kalipha and I smiled significantly at each other. 'Ah, yes,' he murmured, 'thanks be to Allah, all is well now between them.' Farrah caught our meaning for he laughed, a little bashfully, and said to Kadeja: 'We bagged our djinn, and threw him into the river, didn't we?'

We had lit our cigarettes and were settled comfortably when there was a knock at the door. It opened upon Farrah's brothers who salaamed and were, in turn, salaamed as they took their places among us. Tonight was open house at Sidi Farrah's. Upon the arrival of his brothers, a steady stream of men poured into the room until we were a solid mass around the fire-pot. In the rich light of the oil lamps the lean faces gleamed like burnished copper. Kadeja withdrew to the dim region beyond the pillar where the womenfolk huddled, whispering and laughing.

It was bitterly cold outside. Each time the door opened upon another muffled figure, the sharp air burst in, causing the flames to leave their wicks and emphasizing our warmth and simplehearted cheer. The room was blue with cigarette smoke. Kalipha's kif-pipe was passed about and the mawkish fumes of the burning hemp went to the head. Sidi Farrah, looking every inch the sheik, prepared the tea and, as a mark of the occasion, the steaming cups which Boolowi handed around were garnished with roasted chick-peas. 'Are we to have a song, Brother Rashid?' Farrah addressed a curly headed youth who smiled shyly and produced his flute. A place was promptly cleared beside him for the village bard and the audience relaxed with satisfaction as Rashid put the flute to his mouth and Amar, his eyes on the ground, began to sing. The melody was hauntingly monotonous, the theme a favourite with bedouin minstrels. Long ago, sang Amar, some maidens were at play in the moonlight. They scattered in fright as a horse dashed through their game. Like a shooting-star the rider swept from the saddle, seized Germena, the loveliest of them all, and bore her off. Great was the dismay in the *douar*, the wails of Germena's mother found an echo in every black tent. The lovers rode far and fast across the plain. Reaching a pass among the hills at last, they drew up. They were embracing and praising the Prophet when suddenly a lion of shaggy mien confronted them. He invited the youth to dance with him. So, all solemnly they danced, the lion and the youth, in the light of the full moon until Germena's lover, overcome by his partner's foul breath, fell down in a swoon. It remained for Germena to divert the monster and she offered him her necklace. The fragrance of the ambergris enraptured the lion. He was disporting himself with grisly antics when the youth recovered, and, with a single thrust of his lance, ran the lion through the heart. Whereupon the pair, beloved of Allah, proceeded on their way.

And now, Kalipha informed me, it was my turn to sing. *Y'Warda*, 'Oh rose,' brought down the house. My audience laughed until the tears stood in their eyes. They revived to hearten me with gusty *Sahit! Sahit!* (Well done! Well done!) then relapsed until they were helpless with merriment. With such encouragement, my fatuous *maestro* demanded song after song until I had exhausted my repertoire. Still he was not satisfied, for he was making an announcement that caused the mirth abruptly to subside. 'By Allah!' they breathed, leaning forward, all eyes upon me.

The room was suddenly still. I knew what was expected of me before Kalipha turned to me and said with unction, 'And now, my little one, the *Adan*.' This time my ludicrous Arabic provoked no amusement. The silence, that persisted for a few moments after I had finished, gave way at last to murmurs. They patted their chests in token of respect, they clasped my hands, and with fervent oaths touched their foreheads, then their lips. 'Verily,' I was assured, 'thou art, at heart, a True Believer!' This was always Kalipha's big moment. Self-righteousness and pride made his

165

face a shining star. *'B'Araby*, Brother Kalipha, thou hast surely found favour with Allah!' 'May Allah, the all-knowing, exalt thee for thy zeal!' It is impossible to imagine that any reward laid up for him in the seventh heaven could afford my friend more satisfaction than the commendations evoked by my *Adan!* But he shook his head and sighed, 'One does what one can. He causeth whom He will to enter into His mercy.'

Elmetboostah boasted nothing so bizarre as a timepiece, but it must have been very late when the party broke up reluctantly, consigning one another to Allah's care. The door was bolted and, in a matter of seconds, the lamp was out and the six of us wrapped in our burnouses were lying like logs in a row. Boolowi and Mohammed, on either side of me, sharing my blanket, were instantly asleep. The voluminous folds of my burnous enveloped me like a fleecy tent, my head was cradled in a wooden camel-saddle. Through the tiny aperture that served as a window *el Gamar* the moon sent a shaft of white light. For a few minutes Farrah and Kadeja kept up a desultory conversation between yawns, then I, alone, was awake watching the embers in the firepot pulsate and crumble to ash. It may have been hours, it may have been only minutes, that I lay awake. Blackbeetles and fleas in legions seemed bent on consuming me; down the line Farrah and Kalipha snored to Allah. But the crawling of beetles and the nipping of fleas were nothing compared to the acute discomforts of spending a night between two small boys. I was resigning myself to the probability that I would not close my eyes, when I drifted off into a sound and dreamless sleep.

ENTER HABIBA

Kalipha's child was due to arrive in the spring; if not in March, then certainly in April. It was now May, the baby had not come, and I was to leave for America on the 15th.

Hope of welcoming the little Mustapha, or Habiba, did not entirely forsake me until the 12th, when I began to pack. How confidently I had promised Kadusha that I would not go before she was delivered! ('Please God, may all my dear ones be about me when my hour comes,' she had pleaded.) I had changed my sailing date three times in order to keep my promise. Further delay was impossible. More disappointed than I had ever been in my life, bitterly resentful at the meanness of fate, I made ready for my departure.

But the next morning before I was out of bed Mohammed was yoo-hooing under my window. 'Good news, *ma soeur!*' he shouted up at me. 'Kadusha is in travail at this hour!' At the warning pains the midwife had been summoned, and before daybreak Kadusha was escorted to the baths. 'And now, As Allah is our God, she is seated on the chair!' he finished breathlessly. He was on his way to fetch her mother. As he sped off he shouted over his shoulder, '*Allez vite, alors. Ils vous attendent!*' And, indeed, if Kadusha was already upon the natal chair, it behoved me to hurry.

Relief, dread, anxiety, joy—I could not have told what I felt as I plunged into my clothes and hurried through the lanes, where the coloured doors of shops were still shut against the day. I was rushing along the main street dodging loaded burras, carts, and camels, when I heard Kalipha calling me. He and Babelhahj were seated in front of one of the cafés taking their coffees. 'Where are you going, *ma petite,*' he chided me serenely, 'that you run as if pursued by the devil himself?'

'But don't you know? Your wife is on the chair!'

The men looked amused. There was still plenty of time, they said, making room for me on the bench and ordering coffee. Because a woman is on the chair—what does that signify? Good Lord, city women were the limit with their theatricals; their midwives, baths, and chairs! Now the bedouine! They reminded each other of how she drops out of the caravan, has her child, ties it to her hip, then presses on to overtake the others. I stayed only long enough to gulp down my coffee, my hands trembling so with nervous fury I could scarcely hold the cup, and left them still deprecating the hullabaloo of confinement.

Numéro Vingt looked somehow mysterious today, as if hinting, very subtly, of the event that was being enacted inside. I rattled the knocker, but no kop-kop-kop of clogs descended the stairs in answer. I rattled it again, this time a little louder. Nothing happened. So I pulled myself together and let it fall—it made, an awful noise. Then, as there was still no response, I thrust myself against the door. It yielded, shrieking. Prepared for the worst, I started up the stairs. Sounds came down to meet me—sounds that my ears absolutely refused to credit. I stepped into the court.

But this was a party! Here were romping children, a score of women togged in their garish best sitting about in little groups drinking tea! *'Alla-la-een! Alla-la-een!'* all shrilly welcomed me. In the midst of the carnival sat Kadusha. Her face under the bizarre make-up was very grey, her ornamented eyes, sunken and sad, but at sight of me she tried to smile.

The natal chair—pale blue, gaudily decorated with the symbols of fertility in red and yellow paint—has sides but no back. There is a crescent-shaped opening in the seat to accommodate the descent of the child. The chair is ample enough for two and Kadusha was reclining in the arms of her young aunt, Shedlia, who sat behind her, with legs extended. Dangling within Kadusha's reach was an orange rag that was attached to a beam overhead. The old midwife, Ummi Banena, was crouched at her feet. She kept up a droning chant while her hands were busy precipitating the delivery. Just what they were doing couldn't be seen, for they worked under cover of a shawl that modestly covered her patient's lap.

Dazed, bewildered, I was drawn into one of the little groups and plied with tea and fête cakes. In my ignorance I had hoped that I might be able to help! There was nothing, nothing I could do except sit myself among the spectators of Kadusha's pain. She was terribly alone. Even

Zorrah, who had been through this so recently herself, was paying little heed to her daughter, although she held her hand. The liveliness of the chatter did not diminish during those intermittent struggles when Kadusha groped for the rag and groaned 'Ya Mo-ham-mud!' This was a signal for Shedlia to tighten her embrace, for the midwife to invoke with a loud voice the compassion of Allah and His prophet until Kadusha, ceasing to moan and grimace, sank back exhausted.

Jannat smiled at my look of horror. 'Ah yes,' she nodded, twisting her hand in an inimitable little gesture, 'it is like that.' All of the women, with the exception of Ummulkeer and Eltifa, had been mothers many times, and most of them were pregnant.

Still the guests kept coming, blithely exchanging the compliments of the occasion as they doffed their haïks. Solicitude, anxiety, and fear were not to be found at this party. One or two of the women, in contrast to the others, sipped their tea in silence. Inscrutable, equally unmoved by the spectacle—after all, it was such an old story—they epitomized for me the gruesome acceptance that is the women of Islam.

Now a plate was being brought in. It had been prepared by Abdallah, and was covered with hieroglyphics traced in brown syrup. A little water was poured upon it, and when the script had dissolved the plate was held to Kadusha's pale lips. But even the essence of holy writ did not bring an end to her suffering. It was inconceivable that she could bear much more.

In the meantime a vociferous discussion was on, the subject of which was, if I could trust my ears and feeble Arabic, a gramophone! Voices above voices clamoured to be heard. The excitement eventually culminated in the dispatch of Kalipha, who was discovered sitting on the stairs.

My mystification must have been apparent, for together and in turns they explained to me that a pre-natal craving allowed to go ungratified is liable to leave the direst effect upon the issue. Throughout her pregnancy, it seems, Kadusha had longed to listen to a gramophone.

Kalipha had returned with the owner of the instrument. Steps upon the stairs sent the women scuttling to the far wall, hastily wrapping their haïks about them lest they be seen. From the landing the painted horn was extended into the court. Sidi Middib in the doorway, but with eyes respectfully downcast, placed the disk and wound the handle. The thing began to twitter a monotonous falsetto on a theme of voluptuous love-making. The women sat entranced. And, as if the life in her womb responded, Kadusha's paroxysms intensified. She had seized the midwife's head in both hands. With all the strength she could summon she laboured, until, bending forward in the extremity of anguish, she yielded her child.

Before I realized it had come there was a concerted lunge toward the chair. The room was full of hysterical cries and confusion. The black disk whirled on, oblivious. Above the deafening lamentations and praises the voice of Ummi Banena announced, *'B'Araby benáiya!'* ('By God! A girl!') whereupon felicitations, prolonged and piercing, must have roused the long dead, but Kadusha, the colour of death, did not stir. They poked and pinched her, screamed in her ears, drenched her face and head with vinegar, tried in vain to make her drink, and with the first flicker of the eyelids stormed her with congratulations.

Meanwhile the midwife, on her haunches, was trying to make herself heard. *'Weni mousse?'* ('Where's the knife?') she kept shouting. Much dashing about produced a rusty razor, Awisha was sent flying to a neighbour's for a bit of cord, and at long last the tiny entity was inserted into her shirt. But she must wait again until they tore one of Ummi Sallah's garments into strips, for it is propitious to swaddle the baby at first in the cast-off garment of an aged woman. So, all bound in cotton pieces, Kalipha's daughter Habiba was handed up, blinking and mouthing, to be kissed all around, then stowed away in the bed.

The excitement subsided. Sidi Middib went away, the machine on his head. The midwife, having washed her smeared hands, was burning incense upon the fire-pot; her eerie incantation was to exorcise the djinns that all might go well with mother and child. Kadusha, still upon the chair, was acknowledging congratulations and giving directions for the old woman's refreshment. Finally she rose and, without assistance, walked from the court into the room and got into bed, where she sat up arranging her dishevelled garments. As many of the women as could took seats beside her. Kadusha made room for me, insisting, until I too found myself on the bed. And as long as I remained she didn't once lie back but sat up, unsupported, entering into the conversation with the energy of a convalescent of some slight indisposition!

While the midwife was eating in the corner, Ummulkeer and Shedlia cleared room for themselves on either side of Kadusha and began energetically kneading her loins and thighs. When they were satisfied that they had dislodged any djinn that might have lingered there, each of the girls placed a bare foot against Kadusha's cheek and taking hold of her hands they pulled, straining backward as far as they could. Then they pulled her legs. Even a bedouine couldn't have endured these exercises more stoically than Kadusha! The sweat stood out on her forehead and she smiled wearily when they told her that they had done. All that remained for her to do was to eat a small handful of *camoon*, or cloves, for the expedition of her recovery. Some cloves were sprinkled upon Habiba, and after her eyes and mouth were washed out, she was placed at Kadusha's breast. The deep look of love she gave the little stranger as she tucked the nipple into that button mouth!

Her meal over, the midwife did not delay her departure. The guests each contributed a pittance toward the payment of her fee, as was customary; Ummi Banena put her withered lips to the baby's brow and, after a profusion of blessings, went her way. The natal chair would follow on donkey back. As if her exit was their cue, the guests began to don their *haïks*. '*Inshallah mandiksow*,' they told Kadusha in farewell, 'May Allah bless thee and thine.' '*Inshallah farhat Habiba!*' 'If it be the will of Allah, may Habiba marry young and prosperously.'

This photograph shows Dahris Martin wearing a Tunisian *burnous* at the time of her stay in Kairouan, and was taken by the American photographer Louise Dahl-Wolfe in the late 1920s.

Dahris Martin was born in New York state around the turn of the century. She studied at Columbia University and worked for Doubleday before setting off for Europe to concentrate on her own writing. *Among the Faithful* was first published in London in 1937, but with the arrival of American troops in Tunisia during the Second World War, it was taken up and republished in New York as *I Know Tunisia* (1943). Dahris Martin wrote a number of Tunisian tales for children, including *Awisha's Carpet* and *The Wonder Cat*. She met her future husband, the New England print-maker Harry Shokler, while living in Tunisia.